"Genesis poses a huge barrier to you
the Bible and science. To complicat
and often divisive response. This b
to the integrity of both fields, offers a fresh and harm...... , .
an issue of vital importance."

—**Philip Yancey**, best-selling author

"As reverent, conservative, Bible-trusting Christians, Johnny Miller and John Soden enrich the meaning of God's holy Word by showing what Genesis 1 meant when Moses wrote those words. Clearly and humbly, they walk us through the understanding of Scripture that has changed their minds away from the interpretation of Young Earth Creationism. Not everybody will agree, of course: these are deep matters. But after reading this book, surely everybody will agree that there is more than one way for those who love and obey the Bible to understand Genesis 1."

—**Tim Stafford**, writer, *Christianity Today*

"As Miller and Soden teach us how to tell and retell the story of Genesis, they do so not only by their careful research and clear exposition of the text in its Ancient Near East context, but even more importantly, they do so by the telling of their own struggles and stories, which are then caught up into the story of the gospel. Regardless of how one feels about the arguments put forth, the love of Christ put on display is more than enough reason to read this excellent book as the authors earnestly seek to walk along the Way of the Truth that gives Life!"

—**Michael Loren Gulker**, Executive Director, The Colossian Forum

"The authors have courageously tackled a controversial and thorny issue: interpreting Genesis 1 faithfully in the light of scientific knowledge. Miller and Soden walk the reader through the interpretive issues of the Hebrew text and unveil the ancient Near Eastern background to the world of the Hebrews when Genesis was written. They maintain biblical and theological fidelity while effectively challenging young earth literalism, a view they once shared. They trust Scripture completely, while dealing honestly with God's revelation in creation as uncovered by science. This book will be a great help for laypeople and pastors alike. I heartily recommend it."

—**James K. Hoffmeier**, Professor of Old Testament and
Near Eastern Archaeology, Trinity Evangelical Divinity School

"The Church is at a crossroads and is in need of judicious advice—particularly the sort that is provided by this book. Miller and Soden have tackled the important issue of the interpretation of Genesis 1 and have sounded a clarion call for the church to recognize the importance of interpreting in light of the perspective of the ancient context and the Israelite audience. Though one may disagree with individual details here and there, the clearly written, down-to-earth investigation will challenge readers as it offers insights that will help them to confront the evidence and perhaps reconsider their views in healthy, God-honoring ways."

—**John H. Walton**, Professor of Old Testament, Wheaton College

"Since schools no longer teach how to recognize and analyze the classical rhetorical devices, some readers assume that a simple, literal reading is sufficient to understand the Bible. Commonly, they read a passage like Genesis 1 as though it were written in English to them yesterday. And frequently, it is also assumed that the veracity of Scriptures is linked to this type of interpretation. Genesis 1, the account of God's creation of the universe, is deserving and worthy of better interpretive efforts.

"John Soden and Johnny Miller have authored an excellent, readable book that assumes the veracity of the biblical account, as well as clearly demonstrates that sensitivity to genre, rhetorical devices, and historical literary context leads to a more accurate interpretation that is faithful to the original intention of the passage. This is a far superior reading of Genesis 1 than the simple, literal interpretation because it is aware of the Bible's original context and is rooted in the historical, grammatical interpretation. And in the end, it gives a much better answer to the highly speculative, modern cosmologies that confront the faith today."

—**K. Lawson Younger, Jr.**, Professor of Old Testament,
Semitic Languages, and Ancient Near Eastern History,
Trinity Evangelical Divinity School

IN THE BEGINNING...
WE MISUNDERSTOOD

IN THE
BEGINNING...
WE MISUNDERSTOOD

*Interpreting Genesis 1
in Its Original Context*

JOHNNY V. MILLER | JOHN M. SODEN

Library of Congress Cataloging-in-Publication Data
Miller, Johnny V., 1944-
    In the beginning—we misunderstood : interpreting Genesis 1 in its original context / Johnny V. Miller, John M. Soden.
    p. cm.
    Includes bibliographical references.
    1. Bible. O.T. Genesis I—Criticism, interpretation, etc. I. Soden, John M., 1957- II. Title.
    BS1235.52.M55   2012
    222'.1106—dc23   2012017315

ISBN 978-0-8254-3927-8

Printed in the United States of America
3 4 5 6 7 / 25 24 23 22 21 20 19

To our exceptional
soul mates:
Jeanne Miller
Janet Soden

An excellent wife who can find?
She is far more precious than jewels.
The heart of her husband trusts in her,
and he will have no lack of gain.
She does him good, and not harm,
all the days of her life.

PROVERBS 31:10–12

CONTENTS

FIGURES

PREFACE

During our work together on this project, we have grown in our understanding, in our convictions, and in our friendship with each other. We have been friends and co-laborers in Christ's vineyard through our fellowship in the same church for a number of years. We have shared a concern for Christian students who flounder in their faith when challenged with a scientific worldview that conflicts with Young Earth Creationism, and who do not know that there is a biblical alternative that is faithful to the text and intention of Scripture. Our shared commitment to and understanding of Scripture prodded us to join forces to write this book.

Our target audience is students and lay Christians who have a high interest in the creation account of Genesis 1:1–2:4, and who either are unprepared or unmotivated to wade through highly technical material on the subject. We have tried to make our case in terms relatively accessible to anyone willing to take a little time to understand the context and familiarize themselves with gods that are strange to us but were not strange to Israelites in the second millennium B.C. We have tried to keep more technical material in the endnotes for those motivated to pursue the study further. And we do hope many will want to do just that!

Our critics and our encouragers make us better, and we have profited from plenty of both. We want to thank those who have contributed to our motivation and understanding during this project. Michael Murray, vice president of the Templeton Foundation, was the first to see the need and possibility of this work and encouraged us to begin. Among those with expertise in the vast area of ancient Near Eastern studies who have generously shared their thoughts and time are Lawson Younger, Gordon Johnston, and James Hoffmeier. The improvement to the work is to their credit, while any shortcomings are our responsibility.

We are grateful to the administration of Lancaster Bible College, which, under the leadership of President Peter Teague, granted sabbatical time and encouragement for our work. The points of view expressed in this book are totally ours, but the mutual respect of those who differ with us is a tribute to the oneness of the body of Christ. We have experienced that same kind of oneness among our church leaders, who represent a variety of perspectives on creation.

We each have a loving wife—Jeanne Miller and Janet Soden—who has encouraged us in our writing despite the pressures on family time. They have also read through the manuscript and suggested clarifications and improvements that have made it more readable for the less scholarly, but nonetheless committed, Christian reader.

We must also thank friends, family, students, and colleagues who have read through the manuscript and offered suggestions, clarifications, and encouragement.

Finally, we are thankful to our Lord for the privilege we have of pondering the sacred texts of Scripture, of listening to the voice of God, and of trying to make that voice plain to the people of God in our generation.

Part 1

PAST AND PRESENT ISSUES IN INTERPRETING THE CREATION ACCOUNT

Chapter One

ASKING THE RIGHT QUESTION

Johnny Miller's Story

The pastor really lit into me. From the pulpit. In front of everyone. "People who don't believe this literally, don't believe the Bible." He was talking about the days of creation as recorded in Genesis 1. "My Bible says . . ." he repeated over and over. Actually, it was "*My* Bible says . . ." Well, it was really, "**My** Bible says . . ." And he would thump the pulpit with emphasis on "*the first day.*" Then, "*the second day.*" All the way through "*the sixth day.*"

His Bible was the New International Version. As he talked I guessed that he had never compared *his* Bible with the Hebrew Bible. But I was thankful that he believed in the authority of Scripture and the verbal inspiration of the Bible—that every word was inspired by God and therefore that there is no error in what the Bible presents as truth. I believe this too. I just wish he hadn't been so hard on anyone who disagreed with the way he read *his* Bible.

To be fair, he didn't know that he was being hard on me personally. My wife and I were visitors among the thirty or so worshipers in the small Wyoming church that summer Sunday morning. We were on vacation and had searched out a place to worship. I didn't expect to be told that I was an anti-biblical, naturalistic, evolutionistic unbeliever that morning.

But I could empathize, because I was sure I had said similar things myself. In my forty-plus years of ministry, I've served about twenty-five years as a pastor and fifteen years as an educator. For many of those years, I had exactly the same understanding of Genesis 1 as the pastor in that Wyoming church. It was obvious to me that the references to days meant twenty-four-hour days, bounded by evening and morning, and that in the context of Genesis 1–5, the chapter was referring to a creation that took place fairly recently, from 10,000 to 50,000 years ago. I had come to that conclusion through the timely influence of Henry Morris and his coauthored book *The Genesis Flood*.[1]

When I graduated from Arizona State University, like many university students I was awash with doubts about the Christian faith of my childhood. I was confused about the age of the earth, the significance of geology, the authority of Scripture, and lots of other things. I had been raised in fundamentalist churches where the Bible reigned supreme—that is, our interpretation of the Bible reigned supreme. To question our interpretation of the Bible was equal to doubting God and proving you weren't really a Christian. So I kept my growing doubts to myself and just quietly backed away from a living faith.

However, the resurrection of Jesus Christ tethered me to truth. That event stood out as history, and I was a history major. I could not simply jettison history. After a couple of years of spiritual wandering, I returned to the fold and made a mature, all-out commitment to Jesus as Lord of my life. I had lots of questions, even doubts, about the Bible, but I had no doubt about who Jesus was and is.

Shortly after making this commitment, I went to graduate school to study for ministry. While I was at Dallas Seminary, Henry Morris came to speak in chapel. He and John Whitcomb had recently published *The Genesis Flood*, and what Morris said made perfect sense to me. I began to pore over creationist writings. A friend and I put together a one-day workshop on the creationist perspective, and we were invited to present it in many churches and schools over the span of a few years. I also launched out on my own and traveled broadly to speak on creationism.

The age of the earth had not been an issue for me in my youth, because the sacred Scofield Bible notes allowed for an old earth, with a lengthy time gap between the original creation (Gen. 1:1–2) and a proposed re-creation beginning in Genesis 1:3. Indeed, as far as I can discern, the current Young Earth Creationist movement really dates back to the influence of the Morris and Whitcomb publication.[2] But I began to believe that if you take Genesis 1 literally, then you also must take Genesis 2–5 literally, and putting these chapters together with a tight genealogy demands a young earth. That's what I preached from the pulpit, and that's what I taught in my apologetics courses in Bible college and seminary. I could easily have claimed, *"My Bible says . . ."*

But my perspective changed radically about fifteen years ago. One element that contributed to the change was scientific: I discovered that what I thought were watertight proofs for a young earth were highly debatable. I confronted the question of whether God would interject into the world apparent evidence of age if it would deceive people into believing the earth was old. I checked the footnotes of a handful of creationist literature, and found that many of the citations of scientific literature were taken out of context or were impossible to find. I am not a scientist; I am a theologian and a student of Scripture. But I am well acquainted with several godly scientists who love God intimately and are committed to the absolute authority of Scripture, and who also believe in an ancient creation.[3] They confirmed that what I was coming to understand about science was accurate.

Please understand, science does not determine what the Bible means, nor does it determine whether the Bible is true. The latest word in science has never yet been the last word in science. The latest opinion or discovery always stands ready to be modified or discarded by a subsequent finding. Nevertheless, science, like history, can help to challenge questionable interpretations of the Bible, as it did in the days of Galileo, as we will see in the next chapter. It can force us to correct erroneous interpretations.

At the same time that I was beginning to have scientific questions about the legitimacy of the young earth position, I was also beginning to delve seriously into the language and setting of the Genesis account itself, and that was the most eye-opening of all. I realized that all my life I had been reading Genesis from the perspective of a modern person. I had read it through the lens of a historically sophisticated, scientifically

What did Moses mean when he wrote Genesis 1? (Photo credit: Jeanne Miller, courtesy of Bethel Temple, Lancaster, PA)

influenced individual. I assumed that Genesis was written to answer the questions of origins that people are asking today.

But I had never asked the most vital question of all: What did Moses mean when he wrote this text? After all, "my Bible" was Moses' "Bible" first.[4] Was Moses acquainted with Charles Darwin? Or Henry Morris? Or Hugh Ross? Was he writing to discredit any modern theory of evolution? Were his readers troubled by calculations of the speed of light and the distance of the galaxies from earth? Were they puzzling over the significance of DNA? Were they debating a young earth versus an old earth? Would they have had any inkling about a modern scientific worldview? If you agree that the answer to these questions is obviously no, then the logical question is, what was on their minds? How would they have understood Genesis 1?

I have read a great deal of literature debating the meaning of Genesis 1, but rarely do the authors even ask, much less start with, the question that is the most important question of all: What did Genesis mean to the original author and original readers?

John Soden's Story

The question of meaning is where my story intersects with Johnny's story. In high school and college I read Institute for Creation Research literature, assumed a twenty-four-hour day, young earth perspective, and believed that someday all of our questions would be resolved. This has not been a particularly emotional issue for me, but it has held a high degree of interest. I majored in the physical sciences in college and appreciate the explanatory power of a good scientific theory with regard to the data of natural revelation. I believe that the sciences reveal God as a God of order and creativity, among other things.

As I moved into my graduate studies focusing on the Old Testament, I began to see other questions that seemed to remove the emphasis from the elapsed time of creation, and that suggested that the account in Genesis is not concerned with the timing of creation, either directly or primarily, and perhaps not even at all. It seemed to me that the text was not written to answer the question of how long it took God to create but was concerned with the character and rule of the one who created. I began to believe that the text did not require a "seven-day, twenty-four-hour" answer to our modern question.

As my presuppositions about the text were challenged, my recognition of the conflicts between the text and science deepened. I was presented with increasingly complex issues and I also began to realize a renewed force to questions I had easily dismissed before. As Johnny has already mentioned, the questions of science do not determine the meaning or truth of Scripture, but they should cause a careful reexamination of the text and what it actually says, as opposed to what we assume it says. I do not want to believe something merely because I am told that it is true or because I assume it is true. I want to believe what God actually intended and what I am convinced he means in his Word to us.

However, as I studied the issues, I became more deeply aware of a polarization among believers and, at times, a decided lack of civility in the debates on this topic. Like Johnny, I also have been chastened, probably unknowingly, with the comment that if you do not believe in a "literal" creation (young earth and twenty-four-hour creative days), you do not believe the Bible or have the faith of Abraham. The problem is that if I do not have the faith of Abraham, I am not saved (Rom. 4:1–8)! Whether people intended to say this or not, the implications seem clear enough. Yet my greatest desire is to know, live out, and then accurately and adequately express the truth of God's Word.

The issue at hand is not whether God *could* have created the earth in six twenty-four-hour days. Nor is the primary issue whether he *did* do it in six twenty-four-hour days. God could have done it any way he wanted. The primary issue is what Genesis 1 is intended to teach us. It is only a secondary consideration of how the meaning of Genesis 1 correlates with our conception of current scientific understanding.

That is why we're writing this book. We have repeatedly heard that the only reason Christians would not take Genesis 1 "literally" (assuming that means creation in six twenty-four-hour days) is if they are Darwinists, and thus are trying to change Scripture to fit their science. This is not true of us. We are not trying to accommodate either Darwinism or science. Naturalistic Darwinism is built on the triad of chance, time, and progress. The creator God of the Bible knows nothing of chance. Science tries to relate all of the data of the universe to a comprehensive understanding of how the universe came to be and works. We do not believe that Genesis 1 speaks to those issues in the same way. Instead, we believe that it is essential to read Genesis 1 as it was meant to be understood. Only after we see Genesis 1 (and the rest of God's revelation) from the perspective of both its author (in this case, Moses) and its original readers will we have the right to apply it to modern discussions (or debates) about the age of the earth and the meaning of the days of creation. We want to adjust our perspective to read the text from Moses' perspective instead of from ours; if we don't, we'll probably make the same kinds of mistakes that Bible readers made before Galileo.

Countless Other Stories

The stakes in this study are high. Not everyone raised in the church is able to reconcile their biblical understanding and the scientific claims as we did. Ronald Numbers, author of the encyclopedic *The Creationists* cited above, is Hilldale Professor of the History of Science and Medicine at the University of Wisconsin–Madison. He earned his PhD in history at the University of California, Berkeley, in 1969. He was taught Young Earth Creationism in his Seventh-day Adventist upbringing. But during his doctoral studies he became convinced that the earth was "at least thirty thousand years old. Having thus decided to follow science rather than Scripture on the subject of origins, [he] quickly, though not painlessly, slid down the proverbial slippery slope toward unbelief."[5]

This is the silent testimony of many students who were raised in conservative churches, but who surrendered their faith during college because it seemed they had to choose between science and Scripture. Perhaps that wasn't really the choice. Perhaps the choice was between science and a misinterpretation of Scripture, or between Scripture and erroneous science.

Perhaps a better understanding of Moses' meaning in Genesis 1 can point more people toward, instead of away from, genuine biblical faith. Is it even possible to understand Genesis as Moses meant it to be understood? Would this settle all of the debate about the age of the earth and its relevance to biblical interpretation? We will explore these questions together in the following pages.

Chapter Two

WE'VE BEEN HERE BEFORE

There's a great deal of social pressure in some conservative, Bible-believing circles to accept the position of Young Earth Creationism on the literal nature of the six days of creation in Genesis. Both of the authors have been suspected of not believing the Bible because we have doubts that this is what Genesis is teaching or requires. Such pressure is understandable when it comes from a sincere desire to uphold what is perceived as the truthfulness of Scripture.

When Johnny was president of Columbia International University, he received in the mail a listing of Christian colleges that taught Young Earth Creationism, and Columbia was listed among them. He wrote the organization that published the list to say that there were people among the faculty at Columbia who held that position, and that it fit within Columbia's doctrinal statement, but that it was not an official doctrine of the school. He soon received a revised listing that put Columbia among schools that did not believe in creation! For many, it's an either-or position: young-earth, twenty-four-hour-day creationist or naturalistic evolutionist.

We admit that our understanding of Scripture was challenged by science, and some might feel that we have abdicated authority to science instead of accepting Scripture as authoritative. But history has proven that unless we are open to having our interpretations challenged, we will likely be captive to our own assumptions, bound by our culture. Unless we allow outside data and other interpretations to challenge us and cause us to reevaluate our interpretation, we will be locked into our own world and possibly miss God's meaning and intent for the original audience.

The church has been there before, when the official position of the church demanded an interpretation of the Bible that was at odds with emerging scientific understanding. The latest science isn't always right, but neither is the church's interpretation of the Bible always correct. This was true in the case of Galileo Galilei (1564–1642). His story of conflict with the church is an instructive paradigm for today.

Galileo Galilei (1564–1642). Physicist, mathematician, astronomer, philosopher, and inventor, Galileo improved the telescope and championed Copernicus's view of the universe with the sun at the center. He died under house arrest from the Roman Catholic Church because his views on the universe conflicted with the teaching of the church.

Galileo lived during the transitional period from the Age of Faith to the Age of Reason. His era was roughly contemporary with those of theological reformers Martin Luther (1483–1546) and John Calvin (1509–1564); astronomer Johannes Kepler (1571–1630), who plotted accurately the elliptical movement of the planets around the sun; and mathematician Isaac Newton (1642–1727). Galileo himself was a brilliant mathematician, astronomer, and inventor, who improved greatly upon the crude beginnings of the telescope.

Galileo lived in Italy and was a faithful member of the pre-Reformation Roman Catholic Church.[1] The church was dominated by a worldview that could be traced at least to the Greek philosopher Aristotle (384–322 B.C.). Long before there were telescopes, Aristotle had concluded simply through reason that the natural state of matter is to be at rest, and that the heavens are perfection, so all motion is regular. The earth, he concluded, is the center of the universe. The Catholic Church had accepted the views of Aristotle. Therefore, to be a faithful Catholic meant to agree with Aristotle. From their perspective, the Bible was replete with proof.

Yes, the world is established; it shall never be moved. (Ps. 93:1)

And the sun stood still, and the moon stopped,
until the nation took vengeance on their enemies. (Josh. 10:13)

[The sun's] rising is from the end of the heavens,
and its circuit to the end of them,
and there is nothing hidden from its heat. (Ps. 19:6)

The sun rises, and the sun goes down,
and hastens to the place where it rises. (Eccl. 1:5)

The Bible confirmed what people experienced every day. It just made sense. If the earth moved, things would be thrown off the globe, birds would be swept backward, objects tossed straight up would not be able to fall straight down.

As Galileo studied the heavens through his improved telescope, he confirmed by observation that the revolutionary teachings of Copernicus (1473–1543) and Kepler (1571–1630) were true: the earth, along with other planets, moved around the sun. This meant the earth was not the *physical* center of the universe. It was a daring conclusion: "Hindsight underestimates the imagination required to break the grip of an age-old conviction that planets must move in perfect circles."[2] He published his conclusions in 1632 in *Dialogue Concerning the Two Chief World Systems.* This put Galileo on a collision course with the political, theological, and academic powers of his day.

Hindsight also underestimates the courage necessary to endure the attacks of the powerful church authorities of his day, who wielded great power over individuals' spiritual lives as well as immense political influence over parts of Italy. Galileo was elderly and unwell when he was summoned to stand trial for teaching heresy against the settled doctrines of Rome. He was not required to leave the safe haven of the Republic of Venice to stand trial in Rome, but the fact that he did so, risking his life for his good standing in the church, testifies to his commitment to the church (as a youth he had considered entering the priesthood). He faced excommunication from the church—which meant possible imprisonment, but, more importantly, it meant eternal spiritual loss to him as well.

The church found him guilty of holding and teaching the views of Copernicus and ordered him to repent, recant, and agree never to propose further in any manner that the earth moved instead of the sun. Under the pressure, Galileo recanted: "With sincere heart and unfeigned faith I abjure, curse, detest the aforesaid errors and heresies"—namely, "that the Sun is the centre of the world and immovable and that the Earth is not the centre of the world and moves."[3] But even his recanting could not change the truth of how nature works. Galileo spent the last nine years of his life under house arrest for his discoveries and writing.

The people who tried and judged Galileo may look foolish or even evil today, but many were undoubtedly sincere individuals who believed that the revelation of Scripture trumped human observation. They were certain that their (that is, the church's) interpretation of revelation was completely accurate and authoritative.[4] They were concerned to uphold the existence of God.[5] And they were confirmed in their certainty by

We've all adapted our views to Galileo's conclusions. The Andromeda Galaxy is the closest large galaxy to ours, only 2.5 million light-years from our sun. (Photo credit: NASA/JPL-Caltech/UCLA)

centuries of tradition and by the agreement of everyone in positions of authority within their theological and academic spheres.

While there are still fringe groups that insist on a geocentric solar system,[6] most conservative Christian groups today, including Young Earth Creationists, have adapted their views to Galileo's conclusions. We haven't rewritten the biblical statements that seem to say otherwise, but instead we have adjusted our understanding of them. We agree that they are anthropocentric, that is, human-centered, and they report the perspective of the observer from earth; they are not scientifically binding. So we take them as figurative, as observational speech, and not "literally" true.

To come to this point in our understanding of Scripture, a lot of groupthink had to be unraveled. Groupthink is the tendency of a group to come to consensus quickly and to avoid conflict, analysis, and independent thinking in its decision-making process. It results from the pressure of the whole group coming to bear on each individual member. The result is that a group becomes ingrown in its thinking. It pressures each member of the group to conform in their thinking or to become an outcast.

Such groupthink may describe the doctrine-setting process for many religious sects. In order to be part of the group, you have to believe exactly what the group believes. It is the distinctive beliefs, values, or practices that hold the group together and that distinguish them from others. To be part of the group, you have to think like the group. The more authoritarian the group is, the less freedom for independent thought the individual is allowed.

Galileo was the victim of a kind of groupthink—centuries of tradition both in the church and in academia. The church determined what the Bible meant, and no individual had a right to question its interpretation. For the church to change its understanding would have been to admit it was wrong, and had been wrong, for centuries. Such an admission would unravel its own standing and worldview; it would undercut the church's authority and its perception of Scripture's authority. Groupthink isn't always erroneous, but it is powerfully binding and often emotionally threatened by challenge.

In Christian circles, groupthink may apply to the distinctive doctrines that bind together churches and denominations. It may be the way we baptize or the way we observe the Lord's Supper. It may be a distinctive doctrine about the second coming of Christ or a unique interpretation of the book of Revelation. It may even be a literalistic interpretation of Genesis 1 that demands everyone accept the days of creation as literal twenty-four-hour days.

There is a sense of rightness in "what we believe," because we've always believed it, and everyone we know and respect (within our group) agrees that it is right. We take comfort in being able to name some very intelligent godly people who agree with us, and whom we believe would probably not be wrong. In fact, it may be shocking to visit a different church for the first time and discover that people whom you would identify as faithful Christians have different interpretations of the same Scriptures or different ways to observe the ordinances. You may wonder if they really are Christians or if you've been wrong your whole life.

Groupthink also distinguishes cults. Mormon tradition teaches that offspring of the lost tribes of Israel settled in North America and built a civilization here, giving rise to Native Americans. Yet there is no archaeological evidence for this, and DNA testing of Native Americans thus far shows no relationship to Jews or others from the Middle East. The group continues to uphold its teaching, however, because it is a distinctive part of what it means to be Mormon. To the faithful there is no way to disprove what the Book of Mormon teaches, because it is considered an article of revealed faith. The lack of evidence simply leaves one without proof. The only evidence necessary is one's personal faith.[7]

Groupthink influences everyone. It informs our worldview, political priorities, family identity, and spiritual understanding. It has also contributed to great evil in this world: apartheid, the Holocaust, Jim Crow laws, anti-Muslim rhetoric, and spiritual bigotry. People who would never individually harm others get caught up in the identity of the group and approve of atrocious, godless behavior. The only way to break through groupthink is to allow—even to *welcome*—questions or challenges to prevailing beliefs. As Christians, we need to help people think biblically, not just according to a group's perceived authority but because of Scripture's authority.

For the purpose of this book, such healthy questioning includes challenging the belief that the six days of creation were literal twenty-four-hour days and that believing the Bible requires holding this interpretation. It also includes questioning the assumption that Genesis 1 is primarily about the physical origin of an ancient universe. The assumption that a scientific reading of Genesis 1 is the only way, or even a necessary way, of reading the Bible has to be challenged. And the assumption that people who read it any other way don't believe the Bible has to be challenged. Our purpose is not to get everyone to conform to science in their thinking—that would simply be another form of groupthink. Rather, our purpose is to help others seek truth and then follow the evidence wherever it may lead. We believe that the Bible is the ultimate source of truth, but we do not believe that any interpretation is as sacred as Scripture itself. We want a world inside and outside of the church that is safe for Galileo.

Chapter Three

FINDING MEANING IN GENESIS 1 (PART 1)

Does Genesis 1 Agree with Modern Science?

Galileo believed that God had two books from which we could learn truth about his ways and his works: the book of Scripture and the book of nature. Citing church father Tertullian, Galileo believed that all truth is God's truth: "We conclude that God is known first through Nature, and then again, more particularly, by doctrine, by Nature in His works, and by doctrine in His revealed word."[1] He warned that it damaged God's revelation when ignorant people spoke in either arena as if they were experts. Galileo quoted extensively from Augustine, the premier theologian of the church, on this issue: "If anyone shall set the authority of Holy Writ against clear and manifest reason, he who does this knows not what he has undertaken; for he opposes to the truth not the meaning of the Bible, which is beyond his comprehension, but rather his own interpretation, not what is in the Bible, but what he has found in himself and imagines to be there."[2] We do not want to speak nonsense about either science or the Scriptures. With this in mind, how do we come to a conclusion about what Genesis 1 really means?

Galileo believed that God had two books. . . . (Photo credit: Jeanne Miller, courtesy of Bethel Temple, Lancaster, PA)

Issues of Interpretation

The meaning that we must start with when we read any part of Scripture is the author's meaning. The Bible is God's Word to us, but it wasn't given *directly* to us—it was written to other people in other languages in other times. Certainly God intended it to speak to us (1 Cor. 10:11), but our understanding of God's revelation must be understood through the original written and historical context. It cannot mean something different from what it meant to the original audience.

Since it comes to us in languages different from our own, we must always be aware that our English Bibles are translated from Hebrew, Aramaic, and Greek writings. Recognizing that the Bible was written in another language means that we must also recognize that it was written in a different cultural framework for people with a different mind-set. The differences might be minor, or they might be very significant. Most translations are produced by experts in the languages and can be read with confidence, but no translation is perfect (just as no translator is perfect).

Because the Bible comes from linguistic, historical, and cultural contexts different from ours, we need to understand these contexts so that we can correctly understand the backgrounds and nuances of words and statements. The most vital question for the interpreters of any literature (and especially the Bible) to ask is, what did the human author (and ultimately the divine Author, God the Holy Spirit) intend for his original audience to understand when they read this passage? Discovering the answer to this question may be difficult, and at times our answer may be uncertain. "All Scripture is breathed out by God" (2 Tim. 3:16), but our interpretations of Scripture are not.

We know humans are fallible when they interpret God's book of nature, which is why science does not have ultimate authority over Scripture. If scientific propositions truly disagree with a correct interpretation of Scripture, we would propose that it is because the propositions are wrong. Scientists no doubt wrestle with issues of pride as much as anyone else, but they generally are willing to admit when they have been wrong or incomplete in their understanding of the world. There is no benefit in holding out against the scientific mainstream, which discards error as quickly as possible so it can move on to more profitable pursuits.

Humans are also fallible when they interpret God's written revelation. As we saw in the case of Galileo, when science seems to disagree with Scripture, it may be because the interpretation of Scripture is wrong. Just as scientists have to be humble in their claims of what science has discovered, we need to be humble in claiming we understand what Scripture teaches.

The Concordist Approach to Interpretation

How are we to read Genesis 1? One common approach is the concordist approach, which means, essentially, to read the passage as if it is in concord (agreement) with a scientific worldview—namely, the reader's (our) worldview. It is a natural reflex to read our understanding into the Bible, forgetting that it was written for people of a different culture and historical context. For example, when we read in the account of the prodigal son in Luke 15:20 that the father ran to meet him and embraced him, we probably conclude he was a happy father. The original listeners to (and readers of) the story would more likely have been astonished that he was such a humble father, because older men rarely ran in ancient Middle Eastern societies. It was a matter of dignity.[3] Or when we read that Jesus, invited to stay with the two people he met on the Emmaus Road after his resurrection, acted as if he were going farther (Luke 24:28), we might wrestle with whether he was being deceptive. The original readers would have known that in the Middle East you say no to an invitation until you find out whether it is sincere, usually the second or third time the offer is extended. The Bible is an ancient Middle Eastern book, and it must be read from the perspective of those cultures and those eras of history.

Therefore, we should be very cautious about reading our scientific understanding into Scripture. For instance, I have heard it argued that Isaiah 40:22 proves that Old Testament believers, or at least the prophet, knew that the earth is round: "It is [God] who sits above the circle of the earth. . . ." Another argues that the same verse is evidence of the big bang: that "who stretches out the heavens like a curtain" refers to the expanding universe.[4] In fact, the verse is probably referring to the arc of the horizon, not to any concept of the earth as a globe. And the heavens are pictured as hanging above the earth with the stars fixed in place, much as a net with lights in it might be used to decorate a ballroom. God is on his throne in heaven, above all his creation (Isa. 66:1–2).

Young Earth Creationists are one kind of concordist. They read Genesis 1 through a particular set of scientific lenses that assume it presents the material origins of the universe, and therefore it is science. They start with the Bible and read science into it. They believe that Moses teaches that creation took place recently over a period of six twenty-four-hour days. Because they are committed to the infallibility of Scripture, and because they believe that their reading of Scripture necessitates a recent, brief creation, they believe that all science will eventually be seen to agree with what they believe the Scriptures teach.

Old Earth Creationists who try to find evidence for their position in Genesis 1 are another kind of concordist. They read the account through a different set of scientific lenses, starting with science and reading it into the Bible. They believe that the Bible agrees with what modern science teaches and that, therefore, each day stands for an immensely long period of time.

Both views take Scripture seriously, and both believe in supernatural intervention in creation. Both, however, read the biblical text through the worldview of a modern person, not through the worldview of an ancient Israelite. In the end, one or the other may end up being correct, but that is not the point. To understand the original intent and meaning of a biblical passage, we need to place ourselves in the position of the original readers as much as possible. We need to begin with an understanding of the text as it was intended for the original audience in the original context. Only after we have understood it from the original readers' perspective will we be able to examine accurately how it relates to any current theory of science. Sometimes our observations of the world (our science) may require us to reconsider our understanding of the text (as in Galileo's case), because we have not adequately understood the text in its original context.

If Genesis 1 was meant to be read in concord with science, it would be necessary to ask, with whose science? The scientific worldview as we know it, utilizing the scientific method, traces back to about the time of Galileo. That doesn't mean this was the beginning of human interest in nature. Aristotle lived more than a thousand years before Galileo (384–322 b.c.). He believed that "the universe is finite and spherical with the stationary earth at its center."[5] He also believed there were four elements: earth, fire, water, and air. If he had wanted to read his convictions into Genesis, would he have found them in concord? Perhaps, because Genesis 1 begins with the heavens and the earth (air and earth), and the earth was covered with water, and God brought light into existence (fire?). Yes, perhaps he could have forced his "science" upon Scripture. But when the science changed, would it have forced the conclusion that Scripture was mistaken?

Astronomer Hugh Ross is a convincing Christian spokesperson for an old earth. He has amassed a storehouse of evidence for a billion-years-old universe and earth that were designed and prepared specifically by God for a relatively brief period of human existence, in anticipation of eternal fellowship between God and his human creatures.[6] His writings are primers of science read through the lens of a worshiping scientist who truly believes that the providence of God accounts for everything that exists. With this humble approach, he then reads Genesis through the lenses of a twenty-first-century scientist and turns Moses (with the aid of the Holy Spirit?) into a modern astronomer. Would this mean that the meaning of Genesis 1 was actually hidden from human understanding from the second millennium B.C. until the end of the second millennium A.D.? Or should Moses have been able to anticipate modern science? We don't think so.

Young Earth Creationists treat the Bible with the same concordist approach when they read Genesis 1 as if it were science, and then try to make it fit into a scientific framework. They have the additional problem of trying to squeeze science into what they understand from Genesis 1, working against the majority of scientific indicators that seem to point to an old earth. Many Young Earth Creationists agree that the earth appears to be old, but they argue such age is only apparent: "Adam and Eve were created as adults, and would have looked old at the moment of their creation. So the heavens and earth would have been created as a complete system and would have looked as if they were old."[7] The argument seems logical, but if Adam and Eve had been created with thirty or forty years of memories, would this have been deceptive? In the case of the earth, it does appear that the earth has evidence of eons of existence, including the light of stars from millions of light-years away, millions of layers of sediment, and enormous varieties of fossils that go far beyond any Noahic flood. These appear to be enormous memories of the earth's

Light takes 15 million years to travel to earth from the Southern Pinwheel Galaxy (M83) at 186,000 miles per second. (Photo credit: NASA/JPL-Caltech/VLA/MPIA)

past.[8] Tellingly, in a radio discussion between Hugh Ross and John Morris, president of the young-earth Institute of Creation Research, Dr. Morris admitted that to his knowledge no scientist had become a Young Earth Creationist based on science alone.[9]

Ross concludes, "If God guided the words of Moses to scientific and historical precision in this complex report of divine activity, we have reason to believe that we can trust God to communicate with perfection through all the other Bible writers as well."[10] What Ross says implies that our confidence in Scripture is tied to our confidence that the latest science has finally gotten it right, and that the latest scientist has infallibly interpreted nature—without using a shoehorn on either Scripture or science to make it fit. The danger is that our confidence in Scripture is tied to its correlation with the latest theory of science. The problem with this thinking is that science continually changes. While we do believe that ultimately Scripture, properly understood, will accord with science, properly understood, we are not ready to tie God's veracity to our most recent understanding of either one.

This tension is a consistent problem with concordism: the concordist must adjust either Scripture to science or science to Scripture to maintain a consistent material approach to Genesis 1. The concordist position may sometimes be illustrated in a biblical text, or, by coincidence, discovered in the biblical text, but in our opinion it is always being read into the text.

Science, correctly understood, does not need a reference from Scripture to prove it. Galileo did not need to find evidence in Scripture that the earth revolves around the sun in order to confirm his observations. Neither does Scripture need evidence from science to prove it true. We do not believe that the primary purpose of Genesis is to give scientific answers to twenty-first-century questions. If the earth is only about 6,000 years old, scientific discovery will affirm that conclusion. If it is older, biblical silence will not alter that truth. Scientists do not need biblical proof to discover the age of the universe.

We recognize that many Bible-believing people believe that the Genesis account requires a certain understanding of science because of the way they read it. We believe, however, that there is evidence in the biblical text and its context that shows it is not revealing the science of creation. Instead, it is revealing the Creator of science, albeit in a prescientific way.

Chapter Four

FINDING MEANING IN GENESIS 1 (PART 2)

Should Genesis 1 Be Read Literally?

Some people pride themselves on taking the Bible "literally." By this they seem to mean that they believe just exactly what it says. They believe it tells the truth and nothing but the truth. And that truth is the literal truth. Every word says what it means and means what it says.

If this is what is meant by "literal" interpretation, then in fact, no sensible person understands all of the Bible literally. Like all excellent literature, the Bible is replete with figurative language. For instance, the prophet Daniel talks about a "little horn" that grows to enormous size and throws down some of the stars of heaven and tramples on them (Dan. 8:9–10). The book of Revelation describes the Lord Jesus as having a sword coming out of his mouth to strike down the nations (19:15). Jesus said that he is the bread of life (John 6:48), and that whoever eats his flesh and drinks his blood has eternal life (6:54, which is the basis of the Roman Catholic doctrine of transubstantiation).

Most Bible readers understand that these are figures of speech, not to be taken literally. That does not mean they are not statements of truth,

Will Jesus have a literal sword coming from his mouth? (From *Biblia, Ad Vetvstissima Exemplaria* by Haeredes Arnoldi Birckmanni [Belgium, 1570]. Photo/Art Research and Acquisition courtesy of Michael Rotolo, www.rotolomedia.com.)

but rather that the literal truth is to be found in the proper interpretation of the figure of speech; this is a better understanding of "literal." The "little horn" stands for an evil ruler. The sword coming out of Jesus' mouth stands for the destructive power of the truth to those who reject or rebel against it. The bread of life stands for the saving and nourishing power of the death and life of the Lord Jesus.

Understanding Figurative Language

What is the correct meaning of a figure of speech? It is the meaning that the author intended for it to have when he or she used that figure of speech. How do we know what the author meant? First, the context is usually a clue, and the culture is often the key. Second, our normal experience contributes to a correct understanding; when we read that a little horn grows massive, speaks, and acts, for example, we assume that this is not literal because it is so far beyond the pale of normal experience.

Science, then, is a specific kind of normal experience—the experiences of many people tested and qualified in many ways, usually over an extended period of time. So we can assume that if something taught by the Scriptures appears to contradict a verifiable scientific fact, then it is either meant to be taken figuratively, or it is meant to be understood as a miracle.

Another category of sayings that we often take as figurative, though they are not actually figurative in the same way, is observational speech. The speaker or writer may refer to something in the way it was commonly perceived (though we now know it to be scientifically inaccurate), without correcting the common (inaccurate) perception. Instead, the perception is simply used to teach a significant truth or to make a point that does not depend on the scientific preciseness of the observation. Jesus, for example, states that the kingdom of God "is like a grain of mustard seed, which, when sown on the ground, is the smallest of all the seeds on earth" (Mark 4:31). The mustard seed was proverbial for its small size and Jesus used this common perception to make a point. In a similar way, James said, "the sun rises with its scorching heat" (1:11). James' audience did not know that, scientifically speaking, the sun does not rise, but it was their observation that it did. God did not correct this wrong perception (nor in everyday situations do we); instead, he made his point by using their observations and without requiring scientific precision.

Recognizing and correctly interpreting figurative and observational language is relevant to our understanding of Genesis 1 and the account of creation. If we interpret literally passages that are not meant to be taken literally, then we are as inaccurate as if we interpreted figuratively a passage not meant to be taken figuratively. Almost everyone agrees that many figures of speech and many commonly accepted observations are used to describe God's creation. For instance, the Bible says that the earth is established on a foundation and that it has pillars (Pss. 104:5; 75:3). This reflects the way the writer or readers conceived of the world; they seemed to think of the land as a disk, not as a globe. The mountains were at the edges of the disk, holding up the sky.[1] They had never seen photos of the

The Old Testament pictures the universe very differently from how we see it in our modern, scientific worldview. Consider Psalm 104:3, 5: "He lays the beams of his chambers on the waters. . . . He set the earth on its foundations, so that it should never be moved." And 1 Samuel 2:8: "For the pillars of the earth are the LORD's, and on them he has set the world." (Rebekah Fry)

globe taken from outer space such as we have seen; the highest they could go to oversee the earth was up the side of a mountain. It would have made sense to them that this disk, with the waters lapping at its edges, was held up by pillars, set on a solid foundation. But, just as importantly, it was a way of saying that God himself established the world, and he governs everything that happens to it. There was a literal truth behind what we perceive as figurative or observational speech; in fact, the ancient people may have understood such statements as literal reality because of their observations. On the other hand, they may have realized that it was not exactly accurate but was a commonly accepted way of speaking of the world. Yet God did not correct them; instead, he uses their accepted way of speaking of their world in order to make his point.

In Job 38:4–6 God uses some of these same images, and he adds that at the time of creation the morning stars sang together (38:7). Was there really a choir of stars, or is this figurative language for an angelic celebration ("All the sons of God shouted for joy"), or is it a way of saying that creation was a joyful experience? In Psalm 98:8 we read that the rivers clap their hands and the hills sing for joy before the Lord (cf. Isa. 55:12). Are we to believe that rivers and trees literally clap hands in joy, or is this a picture of universal rejoicing in the wonders of our God?

Understanding a figure of speech correctly may clear up an old mystery in Joshua 10:12–14 about the sun standing still. The passage is difficult, both with respect to the translation of some of the terms (the word translated "stand still," for example, could also be translated "be silent") and with respect to what is actually happening. It is clear that the event is miraculous and that God is fighting for Israel (v. 14), but the connection between the sun and moon and the hailstorm is not as clear. Since we know that the sun does not circle the earth, we have a clue that this may not be speaking literally (that is, the sun and moon would not have literally stopped in the sky). One way of understanding the text is to interpret the references to the sun and moon as figurative in themselves, as representatives of the cosmic battle taking place, similar to what is recorded in Judges 5:20: "From the heaven the stars fought, from their courses they fought against Sisera." Or Habakkuk 3:11: "The sun and moon stood still in their place at the light of your arrows as they sped, at the flash of your glittering spear." If the references in Joshua 10 are figurative, understanding the text may be as simple as recognizing that the sun and moon were

Canaanite deities, yet were under the command of Joshua. In Joshua 10:11 Baal is spectacularly shown to be impotent when Yahweh uses Baal's own weapons (the storm and the hail) to destroy more Canaanites than the Israelites' swords did. Similarly, in verses 12–14 the sun and moon stand aside while Yahweh (through Israel) takes vengeance on Israel's enemies. Along a slightly different vein, David Howard proposes that "the words about the sun's stopping, standing still, and not hurrying to go down simply describe the entire day's battle, which ended when the sun did go down," and that "the words about the moon's stopping and standing still are linked with the all-night march (v. 9)."[2]

> God was directing the sun and the moon to fight for Israel in the same way that the stars fought for Israel in Deborah's day (Judg. 5:20), or else they were to stand amazed as he fought for Israel just as they did in Hab. 3:11. We do not imagine that these statements in Judges and Habakkuk mean anything except that God's victory was total and that his majesty is awe-inspiring. Do we properly read these statements as involving universe-altering astronomical or geophysical phenomena?[3]

Regardless of how we understand Joshua 10:12–14, it is not a scientific account. It may describe a miracle of nature or it may refer to a spiritual battle in which the gods of the Canaanites stand by and watch Yahweh win. The context (and literary genre) of a passage will normally indicate if something should be understood as a miracle, and in Joshua 10, the end of verse 13 may favor a miracle ("The sun stopped in the midst of heaven and did not hurry to set for about a whole day"). Regardless, we must see the figurative and theological aspects of this narrative (namely, God using the storm and fighting against the Canaanites with their own deities) or we will miss the point. The main issue of this passage empha-sizes that God listened to the voice of man and fought for Israel, using the Canaanites' gods against them: we have a prayer-answering God in the face of overwhelming opposition![4]

Miracles are not only occurrences that contradict the laws of nature according to the will of God—who created nature and has authority over it—but they also sometimes take advantage of nature, so that the timing and results of natural events are exactly what God providentially determined for the good (or ill) of his people. For instance, Exodus 14:21 says that God used a strong east wind to drive back the waters and dry the land for the crossing of the sea at the exodus. It is probable that a scientist (or even a journalist) could have described what was happening. It may be less probable that a meteorologist could have predicted or explained it from natural weather patterns. But in either case, only the hand of God can explain why that wind was blowing at that particular time, with those particular results. And it is improbable that an unaided wind could have achieved everything that was necessary for the miraculous crossing of the sea.

We believe that there are indications in Genesis 1 that the text is not to be taken literally. If we imagine that Genesis 1 were a modern text, written originally in English within the past ten years, and written to be read with our current worldview, we would have a few very clear options for understanding it. First, if we understood that it was meant to be read literally as a scientifically accurate explanation of creation and the origin of all forms of life, then we would read it as a text written deliberately to contradict much of the scientific teaching and theory of today. It would be clearly anti-Darwinian because not only mankind but also at least some of the animals and birds (Gen. 2:19) were formed directly from clay and given life. The text would contradict the apparent significance of the mapping of animal and human genomes, which seem to show interrelationship between different species.[5] It would contradict generally accepted scientific conclusions relating to the age of the universe and the earth. Were it to be believed scientifically, it would force an entirely different approach to science.

A second option would be to read verses 1 and 2 as grammatically separate from the rest of the chapter. Read this way, the age of the earth and universe would not be an issue because then the text would say nothing about when the heavens and earth were created, but only that they were created "in the beginning." So the universe could be billions of years old, but only recently fully occupied, at least by humanity. The rest of the chapter, in conjunction with chapter 2, would still retain its anti-Darwinian nature.

A third option for reading the text as a modern text, if it were written in the past decade, would be to read it as broadly figurative, using the creation of the world as a launching pad for the rest of the story of the Bible. One would conclude that the account was not intended to be scientific. It is not about the physics of creation but about the theology of creation—its ultimate source and significance.

In fact, the Bible was not written in the last ten years, and it was not written in English. Genesis, specifically, was written more than 3,000 years ago, and it was written in Hebrew. To understand it fully, one must read it first in its original language and try to understand it in relation to its original author (Moses), in relation to its original readers (Israel recently released from slavery in Egypt), and in relation to the culture, worldview, and literary genre of the text. This is an issue in the debate on origins that is often—perhaps usually—ignored by Christians. For those who would ignore it, the meaning of the text is self-evident: "The real question involved in this debate is, Do we accept the plainest meaning of the Bible, or do we insist on a reinterpretation in light of the prevailing opinion of scientists?"[6] The plainest meaning of the Bible? This is indeed what we want to find, but the issue is, the plainest meaning *to whom*? We must start with the plainest meaning to the original recipients.

We believe that understanding Genesis 1 in its original language and setting leads us to conclude that it is a broadly figurative presentation of literal truths; it is highly stylized and highly selective. It does not report history as a journalist might do. Sarna states it well:

> The mystery of divine creativity is, of course, ultimately unknowable. The Genesis narrative does not seek to make intelli-

gible what is beyond human ken. To draw upon human language to explain that which is outside any model of human experience is inevitably to confront the inescapable limitations of any attempt to give verbal expression to this subject. For this reason alone, the narrative in its external form must reflect the time and place of its composition. Thus it directs us to take account of the characteristic modes of literary expression current in ancient Israel. It forces us to realize that a literalistic approach to the text must inevitably confuse idiom with idea, symbol with reality. The result would be to obscure the enduring meaning of that text.[7]

We believe that the text itself leads us to a more figurative approach. In what follows, we identify some indications in the text of Genesis 1 that suggest it was meant to be understood by its original readers in a broadly figurative way.

Indefinite Days 1-5, Definite Day 6

Most translations of Genesis 1 do not accurately represent the Hebrew text when it comes to the numbering of the days of creation. Most translations refer to "the first day," "the second day," "the third day," and so on. In fact, the Hebrew text lacks the article "the" on days 1 through 5. It should read as the New American Standard Bible translates: "And there was evening and there was morning, one day" (v. 5); "And there was evening and there was morning, a second day" (v. 8), and so on through day 5 (see figure 1). It is only when we come to day 6 that the definite article is used: "And there was evening and there was morning, *the* sixth day" (v. 31).[8] This detail of the Hebrew text is significant because it is very unusual. The normal way of indicating the "first" of anything is with the Hebrew word for "first" (the ordinal) and not the Hebrew word for "one."[9] The Hebrew phrase used here is almost always translated and understood to mean "one day" in its other uses in the Hebrew Bible.[10]

Figure 1. The Hebrew Sequence of Days in Genesis 1–2	
1:5	There was evening and there was morning, **one day.**
1:8	There was evening and there was morning, **a second day.**
1:13	There was evening and there was morning, **a third day.**
1:19	There was evening and there was morning, **a fourth day.**
1:23	There was evening and there was morning, **a fifth day.**
1:31	There was evening and there was morning, *the sixth day.*
2:2	And on *the seventh day* God finished....
2:2	...and he rested on *the seventh day*...
2:3	So God blessed *the seventh day*...

The uses of the construction for days 2 through 5 are just as unique. On these days the ordinal numbers (second, third, etc.) are used with the word for *day* without the definite article on either one ("a second day," etc.). In spite of hundreds of uses of the indefinite ordinal with an indefinite noun conveying an indefinite sense, the only clearly parallel usage that is translated with a definite sense is in Genesis 15:16 ("the fourth generation").[11] Again, we must wonder why it is written in such an unusual way if it is to be understood as a simple consecutive twenty-four-hour period. The sixth and seventh days do have the article ("the sixth day" and "the seventh day," 1:31; 2:2–3), although day 7 does not use the summary formula, "There was evening and there was morning, day x."[12] Clearly the sixth and seventh days are set apart as distinct in the listing of the days.

At this point many readers may have already said, "So what? I don't care! It still tells us there were seven days, doesn't it?" The point is that Genesis does not state the sequence like a Hebrew reader might have expected. Instead, it uses a very unusual way of expressing the days and makes a significant change in the last two days. It is as if the writer is telling the reader to pay attention because this is not a normal week. What is the significance of this grammar? Commentator Bruce Waltke suggests, "The lack of the definite article on each of the first five days suggests they may be dischronologized."[13] By *dischronologized*, Waltke means that the days may not be intended to be understood as a linear chronology.

Figure 2. A Comparison of Days 1–3 and 4–6			
God speaks productivity into the desolation		God populates the void with life	
Day	Forming by Separating	Day	Filling with Life
1	Light from dark	4	The luminaries
2	Sky from terrestrial waters below	5	Fish and birds
3	Dry land from water	6	Land creatures
	Vegetation added		Humankind

Instead, each of the days is arranged like a separate photo that is to be part of a collected arrangement on a wall. All of the photos are interconnected in their subject matter, each containing a part of the final whole. Their purpose is to lead the eye and the mind to the most complete picture or pictures. The issue is not *when* the pictures were taken but how they contribute to the overall arrangement and meaning of the display. They are carefully arranged for effect, with days 6 and 7 prominently positioned to highlight the goal of the creation of man and the fulfillment of the purpose of God.[14] The arrangement is not purposeless—each of the photos in the arrangement has essential elements that lead progressively to the climax. There is clearly an intended sequence. But the arrangement may be logical (or theological), not necessarily chronological (or scientific). And perhaps there is even more significance, or a different significance, which we will examine below. The point here is the unique presentation, suggesting to the original reader something other than a normal or straightforward reading of a simple week.

It is easy to notice the careful, purposeful arrangement of days 1 through 3 in conjunction with days 4 through 6 (see figure 2). Verse 2 says that the earth was "without form" (*tohu*) and "void" (*bohu*)—desolate and empty. On days 1 through 3, God speaks the ability to produce or sustain life into that which was desolate or unproductive (*tohu*) through the separation of the elements. On days 4 through 6, he fills up or inhabits the empty void (*bohu*) so that the earth would teem with meaningful life. Both days 3 and 6 are emphasized by two announcements of God's creative word and his approval.[15] But none of this means that this is a scientific description of the order of creation itself. Rather, the structure makes the point that both order and substance in the world originate with the purpose and plan of God.

Evening and Morning Before the Creation of the Sun

Bible readers have long noticed and commented on how having evening and morning before the creation of the sun generates a problem for a strictly linear chronology. A literalist would likely argue that when God divided light from darkness, he created a supernatural source of light to serve until the creation of the sun on the fourth day.[16] One could point to the New Jerusalem in Revelation 21:23, where God is the light and there is no need of the sun. But neither is there darkness in the New Jerusalem, as there apparently was on the first day of creation. We still have to ask the question, however, what this would have meant to ancient Israelites. What would they hear and understand about the creation of light before the sun?

In our scientific mind-set, the presence of darkness and light suggests that the earth was rotating on its axis. "Evening and morning" are ordinary terms that refer to the setting and rising of the sun from the perspective of the earth, clearly a function of the earth's rotation in relationship to the sun. The fact that Genesis 1 presents "evening and morning" three days before the sun suggests that Genesis 1 may not be about literal days and literal stages of creation.

God's Unending Sabbath

A third clue that the passage may intend a more figurative approach is that there is no stated end to the seventh day, God's Sabbath. Day 7 does not include the "evening and morning" formula. It is envisioned as a perpetual day. God has finished his creation and subsequently settles into the maintenance of the world he has created in order to fulfill his purpose to manifest his glory. Isaiah 66:1 pictures him on his throne in heaven as the place of his rest, from where he governs the world.

It is this concept of God's unending rest that informs Jesus' argument with some hostile Jews when he had miraculously healed on the Sabbath in violation of their tradition. Jesus said, "My Father is working until now, and I am working" (John 5:17). The point is that while God's Sabbath never ended, he still continued to uphold the world and especially to do good: if the Father worked on his Sabbath, the Son could work on the Sabbath. Hebrews 3 and 4 refer to that unending rest in its eschatological significance: "So then, there remains a Sabbath rest for the people of God, for whoever has entered God's rest has also rested from his works as God did from his. Let us therefore strive to enter that rest" (Heb. 4:9–11).

The point is that if the seventh day is not a literal twenty-four-hour day, then the first six days probably are not literal days either. But a creation "week" was a necessary framework in order for there to be a Sabbath, in order for God to declare time to be holy, and so he could call people to the regular observance of rest and worship that make our lives meaningful.

Exodus 31:17, the "Refreshment" of God

What is said above about God's rest as a clue to the figurative nature of Genesis 1 is supported by what Exodus 31:17 says about the refreshment of God. This passage is often cited as proof that the creation week was a literal seven-day week: "Therefore the people of Israel shall keep the Sabbath, observing the Sabbath throughout their generations, as a covenant forever. It is a sign forever between me and the people of Israel that in six days the LORD made heaven and earth, and on the seventh day he rested and was refreshed" (Exod. 31:16–17). The argument is that the human week is to reflect God's week. If it is a literal, seven-day week for people, it must have been a literal, seven-day week for God.

However, there is a problem with this reasoning. If all is to be taken literally, then it must be literally true that God became tired and was refreshed after his rest. The verb "refreshed"[17] is used three times in the Scriptures, including Exodus 23:12 ("Six days you shall do your work, but on the seventh day you shall rest; that your ox and your donkey may have rest, and the son of your servant woman, and the alien, may be refreshed") and 2 Samuel 16:14 ("And the king, and all the people who were with him, arrived weary at the Jordan. And there he refreshed himself"). The latter verse makes it clear that it is weariness that requires refreshment. But was God literally weary? Had he become spent during the week of creation? No, but he was describing his figurative workweek in a way that corresponded with human experience, so that mankind would also rest even as God had "rested." God is drawing an analogy here rather than an equation. If we do not understand God's "rest" and "refreshment" to be the same as man's, should we expect God's "days" to be the same?

The Relationship of Genesis 2 to Genesis 1

One final clue to the broadly figurative nature of the Genesis 1 account is the relationship of chapter 1 to the events described in chapters 2 and 3, the account of the garden of Eden (see figure 3). First of all, that there is a relationship between the two accounts is evidenced by Jesus' combination of them in Matthew 19:4–5: "Have you not read that he who created them from the beginning made them male and female [Gen. 1:27], and said, 'Therefore a man shall leave his father and his mother and hold fast to his wife, and the two shall become one flesh [Gen. 2:24]?'" Jesus' usage does not require that the two creation events be interpreted as identical, but it is at least a specific application of a generalized truth—God created male and female, and exclusive marriage is the proper relationship of the two.

In chapter 2, the man is created from clay first, then the garden is planted, and then animals and birds also are created from clay, as well as "every bird of the heavens" (2:19). While the esv translates the creation of animals and birds as a past perfect ("the Lord God had formed"), the footnote acknowledges that the Hebrew does not indicate past. It has the same Hebrew form as the rest of the narrative and all of chapter 1. While the Hebrew can be understood as a past perfect, one has

Figure 3. The Order of God's Creation			
Genesis 1		**Genesis 2**	
Day 1	**Light** separated from dark		
Day 2	**Atmosphere** created to separate the waters above and below	v. 7	God formed **man** from dust
Day 3	Dry **land** and seas differentiated; vegetation (**plants and trees**) created	v. 8	God planted a **garden**
Day 4	**Sun, moon, and stars** created	v. 9	God caused to grow **every tree** pleasant to the sight and good for food
Day 5	**Sea creatures** and **birds** created	v. 19	God formed "**every beast** of the field and **every bird** of the heavens"
Day 6	**Land creatures, man and woman** created	v. 22	God made **woman**

to determine from the context if that is needed. Otherwise, it indicates a straight chronology. In other words, if we were reading this independently of any other text, we would naturally assume that it is giving us a chronological time line for creation.

If Genesis 2 is taken most naturally (chronologically), however, as the creation of all the plants, the animals, and the birds, then it contradicts the order of creation in chapter 1 (the reason the ESV and others translate it as they do and the reason that critical scholars suppose there is a contradiction between the accounts of Genesis 1 and 2 and that they had different authors). Furthermore, chapter 2 implies only one creative day. There is no reference to any other days and, in fact, the chapter begins with reference to a single day (Gen. 2:4 literally states, "in the day that the LORD God made the earth and the heavens"). If Genesis 2:19 could be taken as the creation of a special group of plants and animals, then it would supplement chapter 1, but it would also indicate that chapter 1's creation account is not to be taken as complete. It would be difficult to argue for a special group for the birds, however, if we take the text literally, since it states "every bird of the heavens." Without this possible interpretation, one must argue for another way of harmonizing the accounts.

The point is that everyone who assumes the two accounts are not contradictory but complementary will also argue that the author intended to give a nonchronological order in chapter 2 in order to make a theological point (for example, mankind is seen as central to creation rather than as the climax). If chapter 2 is out of order for theological reasons, why must chapter 1 be in order chronologically? The only reason for this assumption is because it makes sense to us and because we have assumed that the enumerating of the days requires it. If the lack of the article on the first five days shows us otherwise, then a strict, linear chronology of Genesis 1 is not necessarily required.

If the Eden account is meant to be understood as *the* sixth day, then the sixth day has more to it than is apparent in chapter 1: on this day, Adam is sculpted from clay, animals and birds are sculpted from clay (or had already been formed; the verb in 2:19 can be translated "had formed"; note also that 1:20 presents the creation of the birds on day 5); Adam reviews all of the animals in the garden and finds no helper for himself; then he is put into a deep sleep and the woman is created from his rib. This is, of course, all miraculously possible, but it is certainly a different picture of the sixth day than one gets from Genesis 1. The description of day 6 in Genesis 2 has led some people to conclude that day 6 may not, in fact, be a literal twenty-four-hour day, but rather it represents a longer creation day.

The point is that one cannot take both Genesis 1 and Genesis 2 "literally" without creating contradictions between the creation accounts. This is a final clue from the passage itself that it is not meant to be taken literally, or as if it is scientific information. We agree with this judgment as to the nature of the message of Genesis 1:

> It appears that Genesis itself is not interested in giving us a clear and unambiguous understanding of the nature of the creation days. This ambiguity fits in with the overall impression we get

of the passage, that it is not concerned to tell us the process of creation. Rather it is intent on simply celebrating and asserting the fact that God is Creator.[18]

When we come to recognize some of these clues that the original audience would have intuitively noticed, we realize that our naively "plain" meaning was not plain in the same way to the original audience. The details help us read the text more carefully and look for all of the clues the author has given us in order to understand his intended meaning for his intended audience. That meaning was written in Hebrew thousands of years ago, to a prescientific culture with a vastly different worldview. In fact, as we dig deeper, we will discover much more data showing us that the original audience would have heard this much differently than we do and leading us in that broadly figurative direction.

Chapter Five

THE PURPOSE OF GENESIS

Even though the book of Genesis is technically anonymous, we believe that Moses is the primary author of the book. Jesus and others, beginning with Joshua and the Prophets, clearly attribute the bulk of the Pentateuch to him, shortening their references to the first five books of the Bible and just calling them "Moses" (Josh. 1:7–8; Ezra 6:18; Neh. 13:1; Luke 24:27).[1] Two questions about Moses' authorship are pertinent to our interpretation of Genesis 1:

1. Why did Moses write Genesis?
2. And, what were the circumstances of his readers, the people of Israel, when he penned and composed this writing?

The answers to these two questions will impact the way we understand Genesis 1 by helping us to read it as the first recipients of the book would have read and understood it. The best way to explore the answers is through the content of Genesis itself.

Moses' Self-Understanding

Did Moses know that he was writing the first book of the Bible as we understand it? The answer is probably no, but maybe yes. No, because it is highly doubtful that he thought in terms of a sacred story that would stretch out for centuries after him, and that would eventually encompass sixty-six sacred writings over a period of about 1,500 years. But yes, in that he could have been very aware that he was penning sacred writings. At least David, by his own testimony, was aware that the Holy Spirit was guiding him as he wrote (2 Sam. 23:2). So then, why not Moses?

Moses was a prophet, and he knew it (Deut. 18:15–18; cf. Luke 24:27). Genuine prophets were channels of God's communication. God is said to have communicated directly with Moses—"mouth to mouth, clearly, and not in riddles" (Num. 12:7–8). That direct communication was the source of the covenantal laws that were imparted through Moses, and that were eventually written in the Pentateuch. It was also the source of the specific instructions about the tabernacle, and it was one of the ways that God led Israel daily. Therefore, Moses may very well have been aware that God was speaking through him and guiding him as he wrote Genesis and the later books.

This does not mean, however, that God dictated to Moses what he should write, nor does it mean that Moses would not have had sources—both written and oral—to draw from as he reconstructed the history of mankind and, more specifically, the history of the offspring of Abraham.[2] Regarding the historical remembrances in Genesis, there is no evidence that they are the fruit of direct revelation rather than an oral or written tradition: the author never says in regard to history, "The Lord said to me . . ."

The Structure of Genesis

The kind of literature that Genesis represents was not unique to Moses. It was not some kind of heavenly dictation never before seen by humans. Moses was almost certainly prepared by his privileged upbringing and education in Egypt to speak and write in more than one language and more than one style. But he wrote in Hebrew, the language of the Israelites, and in a style common to historical literature: "The Hebrew language was not invented especially for divine use; God spoke

Figure 4. The Author's Structure for Genesis		
Introduction	1:1–2:3	In the beginning, God created the heavens and the earth.
toledoth 1	2:4–4:26	These are the generations [or: this is the history] of the heavens and the earth...
toledoth 2	5:1–6:8	This is the book of the generations of Adam.
toledoth 3	6:9–9:28	These are the generations of Noah.
toledoth 4	10:1–11:9	These are the generations of the sons of Noah...
toledoth 5	11:10–11:26	These are the generations of Shem.
toledoth 6	11:27–25:11	Now these are the generations of Terah.
toledoth 7	25:12–18	These are the generations of Ishmael...
toledoth 8	25:19–35:29	These are the generations of Isaac...
toledoth 9	36:1–8	These are the generations of Esau...
toledoth 10	36:9–37:1	These are the generations of Esau the father of the Edomites...
toledoth 11	37:2–50:26	These are the generations of Jacob.

in a language people already knew. The Bible is similar to other books, and so we should study it with many of the same issues in mind that we have for literature in general."[3]

Genesis is structured by the repetition of the same phrase eleven times: "The generations of . . ."[4] The Hebrew term translated "generations" is *toledoth*, so these recurring phrases are often called simply "the *toledoths*" (see figure 4). The phrase can be translated, "These are the descendants of . . . ," or "This is the history of . . ." The structure shows that one of Moses' purposes was to make clear to the people of God their identity—from whom they descended, all the way back to creation. At the same time, the *toledoth* phrase separates God's chosen people from the rest of mankind. Genesis begins by expressing God's blessing on all of creation, but then shows (beginning in Gen. 2:4) how his purposes were challenged, first, by Adam and Eve's disobedience, and then in increasing measure leading to the flood and the Tower of Babel. In this way, Genesis demonstrates the necessity of God's choice of a particular man through whom to bring his blessing to the world (Gen. 12:2–3), and then it traces his work through the *toledoths* of Abraham's descendants all the way to the then-current crisis in Egypt.

The clear structure of the book is a strong argument in favor of one hand in its writing. Hamilton argues that "the rhetorical features of Genesis 1–11 are so distinctly woven into one tapestry as to constitute an unassailable case for the unity of the section, and most likely composition by a single hand."[5] What is true for chapters 1–11, he says, is paralleled by the structure of Genesis as a whole.

Israel's Historical Circumstances

Genesis traces the history of humanity from the creation of Adam, to the call of Abraham out of Mesopotamia, to the expansion of his family through his son Isaac, his grandsons Jacob and Esau, and then to their multiplied offspring. But even as humanity expands (Gen. 1–11) and Abraham's offspring are enlarged (Gen. 12–50), the focus of the narrator always narrows onto the specific descendant who shoulders the blessing of furthering the promised line: Seth, *not* Cain; Shem, *not* Ham or Japheth; Abraham, *not* Nahor and Haran; Isaac, *not* Ishmael; Jacob, *not* Esau. The history is meant to be read as theology. God was calling to himself a special people to represent his name and so establish blessing on the face of the earth.

Such a people needed a home, a land to call their own. God promised to give such a land to Abraham and to his offspring (Gen. 12:1–3), and God identified that land roughly speaking as the land known as Canaan (Gen. 15:18–21). This land was perfectly situated in the known world to accomplish God's purpose, at the crossroads of the major powers. One problem, though, was that the land was not vacant, awaiting an occupant. It was populated by many other peoples who had their own claims to the land, and their own gods and customs. What right did Abraham's offspring have to the land? If prior possession was indeed proof of ownership, then Israel's claim was the oldest of all: their God was the one who created the land (Gen. 1; cf. Gen. 14:19, 22),[6] and therefore he had authority to grant it to whomever he chose (Gen. 15:17–20; cf. Jer. 27:5; Ps. 115:15–16; Dan. 4:17, 25, 32).

However, to possess the land they needed to be in the land. But when

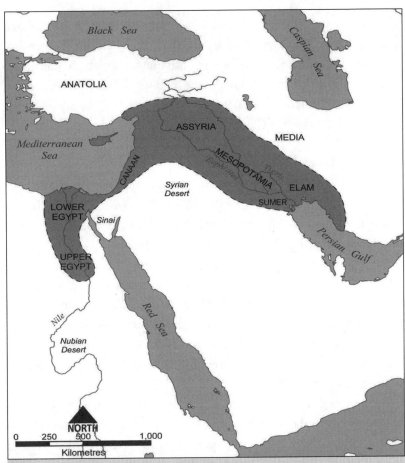

God chose to put Israel in Canaan, the center of the known world, between
the major world powers of the time, in order to establish blessing to all.
(Adapted from Wikimedia Commons)

Genesis was composed, they were apparently not in Canaan. After the
death of Abraham, who was buried in Canaan along with his wife, Sarah
(Gen. 25:7–10), there was a period of severe famine in Canaan, and God
provided for the survival of Abraham's offspring by preparing for them
to be fed and protected in Egypt. The extraordinary rise of Joseph from
slave to Pharaoh's vice-regent paved the way for the fledgling "nation"—
then only seventy strong—to survive, to thrive, to expand, and to unite.

They vacated Canaan in favor of Egypt and food, with God's gracious help.

For approximately four centuries, Abraham's offspring were settled in Egypt. We know nothing about their lives during this period until they were subjected to slave labor toward its end (Exod. 1:8–11). But we can legitimately imagine that they gradually assimilated to their new home. Despite their residence in Goshen, for the sake of trade and survival, they would have been immersed in Egyptian language, culture, and religion. Religion was intertwined with every aspect of life; they would have heard the Egyptians' stories and probably watched their worship. There is no evidence from Genesis or Exodus that anyone was spiritually leading nascent Israel in remembering or worshiping the God of Abraham at this time. In fact, they worshiped the gods of Egypt and took them with them when they left Egypt for Canaan (Josh. 24:14). When Moses is singled out by Yahweh to lead the people out of Egypt, he's prepared for the people to ask about this God's identity: "What is his name?" (Exod. 3:13).

This does not mean that they had lost touch completely with Abraham's God. The midwives who spared the lives of Moses and other babies "feared God [*Elohim*]" (Exod. 1:17, 21). This is the name by which God is revealed as Creator in Genesis 1. It may be that these women knew that murder was wrong because only God could create and give life. Or they may have known the story of Cain and Abel, and God's judgment on the murderer. They feared Elohim, but they apparently did not understand the significance of his covenant name, Yahweh, and perhaps had forgotten him by that name. They did not understand their unique role in salvation history or the way that God would fulfill his purposes through them.

By the end of Israel's four-hundred-year sojourn in Egypt, the people seem not to know that they have either a calling or a land of their own. They need to be reconnected with their God and with their land. At the same time, they need to filter out all of the false concepts of both God and the world that they most likely soaked up in Egypt.

The Reason for Writing Genesis

The connection between the writing of Genesis and the historical circumstances of Israel in Egypt is clear in the concluding paragraphs of Genesis. It reads like a well-written drama. Israel's benefactor, their savior Joseph, dies as a prominent man in Egypt. He has wealth and prestige. He has an Egyptian wife and children. He would be embalmed and buried in style, according to Egyptian hope and custom. And yet Joseph looks beyond his earthly circumstances to the promise that God had given to Israel through its patriarchs: "God will visit you and bring you up out of this land to *the land that he swore to Abraham, to Isaac, and to Jacob*" (Gen. 50:24, emphasis added). For the first time, the names of the three patriarchs are used together, and it happens in conjunction with God's promise of the land.

Based on this promise, Joseph instructs his brothers to carry his bones to Canaan and to bury him there (Gen. 50:25). His last words read as a statement of profound faith and commitment to Israel's God. They also read as an unfinished mandate.

And that is our clue to the immediate circumstances of Israel and the crying need for the book of Genesis. It was written for the people of God after their exodus from Egypt to (re)acquaint them with the God of their fathers—Abraham, Isaac, and Jacob—and with his calling on their national life, giving them a purpose (to bring blessing to the nations) and a future in a land (the physical platform from which to show the nations the source of blessing; Gen. 12:1–3). He was the creator God who had made the land and all that was in it; the God who had defeated the gods of Egypt during the ten plagues; the God who would defeat all other gods, beginning with those of the Canaanites. Therefore, it was time to pursue the mandate of Joseph and the promises and purposes of God by moving on to claim the land. As they heard Moses' words read to them during their wilderness trek, they could glance at the coffin in their midst carrying the bones of Joseph (Exod. 13:19) and be reminded of his faith, of God's promise, and of their mandate to claim the land in the name of the Creator God and

Covenant God, the God of Israel and of all the world. It was only in this way that they could be a kingdom of priests as God's holy nation and mediate the blessing of God to a dark and needy world (Exod. 19:5–6).

Chapter Six

WHAT DOES IT MEAN TO WHOM?

A Guide to Proper Interpretation

Have you ever used an old saying and then suddenly realized that you were not sure what it meant? I (John) can remember using the phrase "sweating like a pig" to mean sweating profusely. Because it was a common simile, I naturally assumed that pigs must sweat a lot. Unfortunately, I was then informed that pigs do not sweat (and I later learned that they have a different kind of sweat glands, which are not for cooling the body). Why would so many people use an illustration that was so obviously a poor analogy? Why did anyone ever choose pigs if they do not even sweat, or at least not enough to notice? Now, what "everybody knew" seemed contrary to fact and totally illogical.

Conducting a little informal research, both on the Internet and in person, I found that people only guess at the origin of the phrase and a resolution for its apparent conflict with reality. Most suggest that the phrase originated simply because people who don't know anything about pigs assume they must sweat because they stink. Someone suggested that it was from a pig roast when the fat would drip off of the roasting body. Someone else suggested that it actually means the opposite of what we take it to mean: that the person actually isn't sweating at all because, like a lazy pig, he's not exerting any effort. A final suggestion from various sources is that it comes from the smelting of iron. The iron that comes out of the smelting furnace is called pig iron, either because of the sucking sound as the iron flowed into sand channels for cooling or because the newly formed round runners of iron look like piglets snuggled up to a sow. As the "pigs" cooled, the air would get very warm and the humidity would reach the dew point, at which time it would begin to condense on the cooled pig iron.

Now I have not done the depth of research required to confirm which of these explanations is actually correct, or if there is yet another actual basis for the saying, but my early dilemma with the saying does illustrate the way we sometimes read Scripture. We assume something to mean what seems plain to us. Suddenly, however, we may see it with new eyes. We may discover that it is impossible to understand familiar words the way we had assumed, or that in the original context they did not at all mean what we had thought. All of a sudden we have to ask, "What did that say? What does it mean?"

Seeing Things Our Way

I have had similar experiences with Scripture. I remember as a young believer thinking that in order to "love" God (Deut. 6:5, "You shall love the LORD your God with all your heart"), I had to feel a certain way. My problem was that I didn't always feel the way I thought love should feel. It was both a relief and a challenge to learn, on the basis of the language and culture of the Old Testament, that to "love" a king in the ancient Near East was equivalent to expressing loyalty to him. It meant to submit one's will and plans to him, regardless of feelings. God used the expression for Israel (and us) to teach the people how to respond to their heavenly king. In addition, the Israelites didn't think of the "heart" as the seat of emotions. Rather, in the ancient Near East "heart" referred to the thought and will, the place of decision making.[1] The Bible did not require Israel (or me) to *feel* a certain way about God but to be absolutely loyal to him in every act and choice. When I learned this, I was gripped by the totality of God's demands on my life.

When we study God's Word, over time we realize that the intent of the author may be different from what we intuitively understand in a contemporary context. The more we learn about the ancient Near East, the more we are confronted with the perspective of the original audience. We learn to reflect on how God spoke to a specific people in a specific time according to their understanding and presuppositions, with their language, culture, and history in view. We come to understand that we cannot hear the Word from the perspective of the original audience if we don't explore their world—or at least have someone share that world with us. It takes work to find out the original context of a document that is thousands of years old. And then, when we do get a glimpse into the original setting, we start to see the literature and the world as the ancient audience would have. Even then, sometimes we still do not have enough information about the original context to assert a particular interpretation dogmatically.

Figure 5. The Process of Interpretation
What does it say (observation)?

• What is actually there?
    • What is not actually there?
    • Details, details, details . . .

What does it mean (interpretation)?

• What is clearly intended by those details?
    • What is probable given the various contexts in which these details are set?
    • What is possible in this context?
    • What is unlikely in this context?

How does it fit together (correlation)?
• How does this passage relate to other passages?   • How does this theology relate to the rest of Scripture?
How should I respond (application)?
• What genuinely comparable situation does this apply to in my life?   • How does this apply in light of my relationship with God through what Christ has done in his death, burial, and resurrection?

While most of us will have to leave such background work to scholars and hope to glean from their linguistic and cultural expertise, we are still responsible to understand the principles behind the correct interpretation and application of the biblical text, so that we grow in accurately understanding what it does say—and what it does not say (see figure 5). We do not want to force the Bible to say something that it does not mean to say. Good commentaries and other scholarly works can help us with the historical, cultural, and linguistic contexts of Scripture. Providing such help with Genesis 1 is our desire in writing this book.

Seeing Things Their Way

Historical and cultural backgrounds are crucial to the correct interpretation of this narrative. What do we need to understand about the text's background to help us interpret it accurately? What questions help us understand what Moses (and God) intended to say? How can we hear what Israel would have heard?

Let's start with the last question:

How can we hear what Israel would have heard?

This is the most crucial question. What did the account mean to the Israelites coming out of Egypt? To begin understanding these bigger questions, we can try to answer more specific questions:

- What went through the Israelites' minds as they listened to Genesis 1? What images did it raise from their background? How did the Israelites relate this narrative to what they already knew as a result of growing up in Egypt?
- How did the narrative impact their expectation for following God throughout the Sinai peninsula and into Canaan?
- How did Genesis 1 prepare the Israelites for the theology and religious activities they would encounter in Canaan, including those that came from Mesopotamia? How did Genesis 1 prepare them

to represent Yahweh? How did it introduce them to their covenant responsibilities as seen in the rest of the five books of Moses?

- How did the creation account impact the general religious understanding and worldview in which the Israelites were immersed and by which they were certainly influenced as citizens of the ancient Near East?

- What historical and cultural background informs our understanding? Have we assumed a modern (scientific?) context with our own experience and presuppositions as the standard? Is our understanding intended by God or assumed because of our assumptions, worldview, or prejudices?

Some questions about the biblical creation narratives have been asked for a long time, and the observations in the previous chapters may bring some of these to mind and more. You may have assumed you understood the plain meaning (pigs sweat!). On the other hand, you may discover that there is more in the original context than meets the eye (pigs really don't sweat!), but you are not sure what the solution is or how to find it.

Some questions can be answered only by understanding the original language. Other answers may depend upon understanding figures of speech. Historical, cultural, literary, and theological backgrounds will give further insight. Even after considering all this background information, difficulties may remain until we gain further insight into the contexts.

Applying this questioning process to Genesis 1 was significant in challenging our own inadequate understanding. We each once assumed that the phrase "without form" described a shapeless mass. But when we were challenged to understand the Hebrew phrase in its context rather than assume our interpretation of an English translation, we discovered that the Hebrew actually describes something that is desolate or unproductive, not something shapeless.[2] Our assumption was about the shape of the globe, or the shape of the mass on the globe, but in reality, the phrase refers to the earth's capacity to support life. Yet, as we shall see, even this understanding does not exhaust the significance of the phrase in its historical context. Why would God choose to describe the beginning of the earth with these particular features: desolate, empty, dark, and watery (Gen. 1:2)? Why are they significant? What are they telling us and why? Why not begin with galaxies or with the formation of matter itself? What did this phrase mean to the Israelites—or was Moses teaching them something altogether new?

Genesis' description of the "first day" of creation adds more questions: How do you separate light from darkness? What was the state of things before light and darkness were separated? Why does Scripture point out that God called the light "day" and the darkness "night"? When we compare day 1 with day 4, we add questions that have perplexed Bible students for centuries: Why did God create light before he created the sun, moon, and stars? What does this mean and how can it be?

On the "second day," God separated "the waters that were under the expanse from the waters that were above the expanse" and made the "expanse" to go in between (Gen. 1:7–8). This detail, combined with a literalistic reading of the text, has occasioned some creative understandings. Does this indicate that originally there was extra water somehow stored above the atmosphere in a sort of vapor canopy that was subsequently released to make the great flood? Psalm 148:4 would argue against such a theory, since the psalmist understood there to be water still above the heavens (expanse?). So how should we understand the waters above the

---

Figure 6. Questions to Ask About Genesis 1

- Why does the story start with a desolate, empty, dark, and watery earth?
- How do you separate light from dark?
- How could there be light before the sun, moon, and stars? What did God create?
- What is the "expanse" with the waters above it?
- What is the "one place" where the waters were gathered?
- Why does Genesis 2 talk of the animals being formed from dust when Genesis 1 says they were spoken into existence?

expanse? Is Moses giving some information that we need to correlate scientifically?[3]

As we carefully read through the six days of creation, the questions only multiply (see figure 6). What does it mean that the waters are gathered into one place? If we look at our globe, how does the water only end up in one place? Why does Genesis 1 suggest God spoke the animals into existence, but Genesis 2 says he made them from dust like he made man? On and on the questions go. Some seem easier and some harder. Some seem picky, while others seem intuitive. But *are* they either picky or intuitive?

How did God intend Israel (and us) to hear Genesis 1? The account teaches both them and us about our God. It seems to focus on the theology of creation, not the mechanics of it. As we will see, there were issues at work that aren't apparent to us in our context, but that the ancient Israelites would have clearly understood in their historical and cultural context. The starting point for creation in 1:2 would have been both significant and obvious for Israel, and the resulting impact of the account would have been a complete paradigm shift for them—a major revolution from their prevailing views of the gods, the world, and their relationships with each other. In fact, any answers we suggest to all of the questions we have raised need to be influenced by Israel's context. As we understand Israel's context better, we should understand the answers to these questions better.

The tendency is to try answering such questions from a twenty-first-century perspective rather than from the original ancient Near Eastern perspective. Just as with sweaty pigs—we think of real pigs instead of pig iron, if indeed that is the reference. Just as with the command to love God—we understand an emotional response instead of the choice of loyalty. So also with Genesis 1, we can be unconsciously locked into the twenty-first century A.D. and totally miss the meaning for the fifteenth or thirteenth century B.C. Does it matter?

All Scripture is breathed out by God and profitable for teaching, for reproof, for correction, and for training in righteousness, that the man of God may be competent, equipped for every good work. (2 Tim. 3:16–17)

While it does not really matter for a casual expression, it is very significant for God's Word if we believe it is written to instruct us (1 Cor. 10:11). We want to set aside our own assumptions and know what God intended.

If the original edition of Genesis was presented to Israel after their exodus from Egypt, and if it was written in an early form of the Hebrew language to people who had lived hundreds of years in Egyptian culture, then we should expect it to reflect a concept of the universe and a worldview different from ours. We should not assume, without examining the cultural context, that we understand figures of speech or allusions to common motifs, beliefs, and theological positions of their day. We should, however, expect to find in the account theological connections to Israel's cultural context, whether by way of borrowing, polemic, or apologetic. If Abraham came from Mesopotamia, we might also expect some religious influence from Mesopotamia. And if his descendants had spent time in Canaan before Egypt and expected to be living there, we would also expect to find some correlation to their experiences there. One might even expect to identify common beliefs across the ancient Near East. An exploration of the creation accounts of Egypt, Mesopotamia, and Canaan will provide us with insight into what the Israelites understood because it will reveal the context from which they developed their worldview, the worldview that God was addressing in Genesis.

The ancient world, as represented by texts from Egypt, Mesopotamia, and Canaan, presents significant parallels with the biblical account of creation, which suggests that the author was arguing against the worldview inundating Israel while defending the uniqueness of Yahweh. The chapters to follow in part 2 will explore some of the parallels between Genesis 1 and Israel's world and define some significant differences. In the process, the ancient Near Eastern context will inform our understanding and help us formulate answers to the significant questions of the text.

THE CREATION ACCOUNT IN LIGHT OF ITS ANCIENT HISTORICAL AND CULTURAL CONTEXT

Chapter Seven

GENESIS 1 COMPARED WITH THE EGYPTIAN CONTEXT

I f you had grown up in India, even in a Christian home, you would have been influenced by Hinduism. You would have been exposed to the idols on every street corner, you would have become used to cows wandering the streets, and you may have had serious questions about Hindu beliefs, especially if you had good friends who were Hindu. In the same way, if the offspring of Abraham had spent four hundred years in Egypt, certainly they would have been exposed to Egyptian religion, including Egyptian beliefs about creation. In fact, Joshua 24:14 tells us that long after the exodus Israel still had Egyptian gods in their pantheon:[1]

> Now therefore fear the LORD and serve him in sincerity and in faithfulness. Put away the gods that your fathers served beyond the River and in Egypt, and serve the LORD.

What, then, might Israel have learned (and believed) from the Egyptians about creation, and how would it relate to what Moses wrote in Genesis?

There is no single Egyptian account known to date that describes the complete Egyptian perspective on creation. Instead, we have to put together a mosaic of bits and pieces recorded in various documents. These documents represent a mixture of times and theologies (covering more than two millennia), many of them in tension with one another, a situation that did not seem to bother the Egyptians. Determining the Egyptian perspective on creation is like putting together a single picture from a dozen different jigsaw puzzles in which each puzzle is a picture of a different artist's rendering of something no one has ever seen.[2] Yet, it works. As James Allen states, "Despite differences in age and origin, imagery and subject matter, these sources all reflect an understanding of creation that was remarkably consistent throughout the 2,300 years of history they span."[3] The creation of the universe, as the Egyptians conceived of it, then, happened something like this:

Beginnings According to Egypt

The starting point: Before the beginning of creation, there was only an infinite dark, watery, chaotic sea. There was nothing above the sea or below the sea—the sea was all there was. Immersed in the sea, Atum (or Re or Amun or Ptah), the creator god and source of everything, brought himself into existence by separating himself from the waters.[4] Egyptian cosmologies that view Amun as the creator, or even as one of the four initial qualities of the precreation matter (watery, unlimited, dark, imperceptible) from which creation emerges, would then also understand the wind to be present in the water, because Amun was also god of wind.[5] Since Atum, Amun, and Re are all connected with the sun, light was then in existence, even though the sun itself had not yet risen.

The means of creating/initial creation: While several means of creation are used interchangeably in the Egyptian accounts (including sneezing or spitting and masturbation), in many accounts Atum (or one of the other gods noted above) spoke the universe into existence. This new creation (or the "universe" as conceived by the Egyptians) began with the separation of the waters to create the atmosphere (a bubble of air, known as the god Shu, in the midst of this endless mass of water).[6] Atum's command separated the surface of the waters in the sky (*Nut*) from the earth

Egyptians pictured the universe much differently than we do in our modern worldview. (Rebekah Fry)

(*Geb*). The waters receded and the first mound of earth appeared. The sun (*Re*), already in the waters (*Nun*) before the separation of the atmosphere,[7] rose for the first time as the main event of creation. And so the basic universe was formed—a bubble of light,[8] air, earth, and sky in the continuing infinity of dark, motionless water.

A universe of gods: The universe was actually composed of thousands of gods (all of which were part of Atum; see figure 7) in the Egyptian understanding, because "all the elements and forces that a human being might encounter in this world are not impersonal matter and energy but the forms and wills of living beings—beings that surpass the merely human scale, and are therefore gods."[9] Into the universe, Atum commanded the creation of plants and animal life, Re formed man as his image, or Khnum fashioned man on a potter's wheel with the breath of the god (Re or Hekat or Aton) giving life to the image. In some accounts, man springs from the tears of the eye of Atum (the sun).

The Egyptian worldview was dominated by equating every aspect of creation with some deity. (Suzanna Vagt)

Order and rest in the end: After speaking into existence the "universe" and its millions of gods with their towns, shrines, and offerings, Ptah rested with everything in order.[10] This description of creation events, found in the Memphite Theology, ends with one final statement: "So were gathered to him all the gods and their ka's[11] as well, content and united in the lord of the Two Lands."[12] This final line identifies Ptah as king,[13] which not only shows the significance of the cosmogonies for ancient Egypt but also parallels the significance for Israel, as we shall see.

In Egyptian theology, all of creation was done in a single day, which was called "the first occasion."[14] At the end of the day, the sun traveled through the Duat (the Egyptian underworld) and fought the enemies of order to arise victorious the next day. Each succeeding day reenacted the creation event:[15] the sun had won its victory over the enemies again and begun a new day of order.

Figure 7. Gods of Egypt	
Amun	• a deity of Thebes • self-created creator deity, god of wind or breath • sometimes merged with Re as Amun-Re and connected with the sun, creator of man
Aten/Aton	• the sun disc • the creator and giver of life • later became the focus of Pharaoh Akhenaten's attempt to force worship of only one god in Egypt (14th century B.C.)
Atum	• a deity of Heliopolis who was connected with Re as Atum-Re • a sun god and self-created creator who made gods, plants, animals, and man (from his tears)
Geb	• a deity of Heliopolis • god of earth • married to Nut, the sky goddess
Hekat	• a deity of Elephantine • goddess of fertility • wife of Khnum • animated man with her breath
Khnum	• a deity of Elephantine • god who was the source of the Nile • creator of mankind on a potter's wheel from clay
Nun	• a deity of Hermopolis • god of the primordial waters, the source of all that becomes creation
Nut	• a deity of Heliopolis • goddess of the sky and heavenly bodies • wife of Geb
Ptah	• a deity of Memphis connected with the primordial mound • the creator who called the world into being • patron of artists
Re/Ra	• a deity of Heliopolis • a sun god and creator who created man as his image and animated with his breath
Shu	• a deity of Heliopolis • a personification of air who held his daughter (Nut, the sky goddess) and separated her from his son (Geb, the earth god)

Initial Considerations of Beginnings According to Egypt

An initial impression of the Egyptian literature highlights how different these accounts seem from the biblical account in Genesis. The worldview described above, in which every force has a will and so is a god, runs completely contrary to the perspective of creation that we have grown accustomed to in the Pentateuch—understood from our worldview. We should not downplay the differences. Considering the accounts of Egypt highlights the contrasts between Egyptian views and Yahweh's self-revelation to Israel through Moses.

Yet it is instructive to ask, why are there are so many similarities? While the differences show a dramatically different worldview and conception of deity, the similarities help us understand something of the purpose of Moses in writing Genesis.

Unfortunately, the lack of a comprehensive Egyptian narrative of the whole of creation (as noted above) makes understanding either the differences or the similarities more difficult. For the most part, Egyptian creation documents consist of brief statements and allusions, scattered among many inscriptions (Pyramid Texts, Coffin Texts, the Book of the

The Shabaka Stone records the Memphite Theology as it was copied and preserved during the reign of Pharaoh Shabaka in the eighth century B.C. (Photo credit: James Hoffmeier, courtesy of the British Museum)

Dead, and other inscriptions).[16] The most extensive descriptions occur in the Memphite Theology and the Hermopolitan Cosmogony.[17] However, not having a complete picture of the Egyptian backdrop to compare to Genesis, we still have a number of significant parallels that help us relate Israel's literature to its surrounding culture and help explain why and how its thinking needed to be corrected. Since the differences are so many and so striking, we will first focus on some of the similarities and then in the next chapter, we will summarize the differences.[18]

Initial Conditions of Creation

Genesis 1:2	Formless, void,[19] darkness, deep
Egypt	Watery, unlimited, darkness, imperceptibility[20]

Allen summarizes the general Egyptian understanding of the world:

> Together, sky, land and Duat (or underworld) comprise the world of the ancient Egyptian—a kind of "bubble" of air and light within the otherwise unbroken infinity of dark waters. These elements form the background to the Egyptian understanding of the cycle of life and human destiny, determined by the daily drama of sunset and sunrise. *They are also the starting-point for all Egyptian speculation on the origins of the universe.*[21]

As the Egyptians understood creation, it was the bringing into existence of a "bubble" of light and life in the midst of the "unbroken infinity of dark waters." There was no speculation on the origin of the dark watery chaos—it was preexisting and seemingly endless. This sounds very similar to the description in Genesis 1:2, the conditions out of which God brought forth his good creation. Both scenarios begin with only dark water. There is no life and no ability to produce life. In each description the cosmos is a waste place: a desolate, dark, empty, watery mass. Even though the details of the story are very different, creation as

As Egyptians understood creation, it was the bringing into existence of a "bubble" of light and life in the midst of the "unbroken infinity of dark waters." (John Soden)

described in Genesis 1 has the same starting point as the Egyptian accounts of creation.

The relationship of Genesis 1:2 to 1:1 and 1:3 has long been a matter of debate. Among many options that are beyond the scope of short summary, two are most significant here. Some people argue that verse 1 presents the creation of all things out of nothing and verse 2 presents a subsequent time. Most of us probably assumed this perspective when we read the chapter for the first time: in verse 1, God created the universe without all of the details in place that will come in the following narrative; in verse 2 focus shifts to the earth, and in verse 3 God begins creating the universe as we now know it. One problem with this perspective is that many assume that God must have initially created only one isolated planet, because the sun, moon, stars, and the rest of the universe do not seem to exist until day 4. Thus, the initial creation could not have had our current laws of physics since most of our universe did not exist. Some long-day proponents try to solve this problem by assuming that the sun, moon, and stars were there, but could not yet be seen because of an opaque atmosphere.[22]

A second view fits the exegetical data better. The similarity of structure at the beginning of chapter 1 (vv. 1–3) and the beginning of each *toledoth* section in Genesis (see, esp., 2:4–6) seems to indicate that just as each *toledoth* begins with a summary of the section to follow, so also Genesis 1:1 is an initial summary of the section to follow, rather than serving as a record of the initial creation of everything. Genesis 1:1 gives a general statement, which will then be described in relation to the relevant parts.[23] Genesis 1, then, presents creation as starting with the qualities listed in verse 2, similar to the Egyptian perception. By saying this, we are not suggesting that God did not create everything out of nothing. We believe that the Scriptures clearly teach that he did (John 1:3; Col. 1:16; Heb. 11:3). Genesis is simply not speaking to that issue. Genesis seems to begin precisely where the Egyptian accounts begin.

We are also not suggesting that Moses merely borrowed from Egypt. Rather, we are suggesting that Moses is starting with the Egyptian assumptions about creation to correct Israel's theology of creation and not their way of talking about creation. Moses seems to begin with a starting point that Israel would have already accepted.

If theological correction was indeed Moses' (and God's) goal for Israel, then Genesis 1 paints a picture of creation different from what most of us have assumed from our reading. Instead of starting with a globe covered completely with water and floating in dark, empty space, Moses starts with the common ancient Near Eastern assumption of limitless water, without any concept of a globe.[24]

| Genesis 1:2 | "The Spirit of God was hovering over the face of the waters" |
| Egypt | The god of wind/breath on the waters[25] |

Amun, Egypt's creator and god of wind or breath. (Photo credit: Jeanne Miller, courtesy University of Pennsylvania Museum of Archaeology and Anthropology)

For this parallel between the Spirit of God and the god of wind/ breath, Sayce draws from the Hermopolitan version of creation, because Amun (god of wind or breath) was among the first of the gods, floating on the deep, and his breath was "the power which had infused motion and life into the primeval chaos."[26] Hoffmeier supports Sayce's argument, noting that Amun had been the god of wind.[27] The Hebrew term translated "Spirit" in Genesis 1:2 can also be translated "wind," and so the NRSV translates, "a wind from God swept over the face of the waters."[28] One difficulty in this passage is determining which meaning the author intended in this context. What would the ancient audience have understood? While the ancient Near Eastern context, including Mesopotamia (see chapter 9), would suggest "wind" and the previous descriptions of the darkness and deep reinforce this, the following description of creativity and the reference to the Hebrew 'Elohim, either personally as "God" or as a superlative meaning "mighty," would suggest "Spirit." One attractive solution recognizes the possibility of double entendre—intentional ambiguity—in the reference, suggesting the powerful working of God in creation.[29] In its historical setting, Israel may well have assumed a wind at creation, but in Genesis 1 the wind is directed by the careful, personal working of a sovereign God, and it comes very close to the concept of the Spirit of God at work.

Means of Creation

Genesis 1:3, 6, 9, 11, 14–15, 20, 24	God creates by divine command
Egypt	Atum (or Ptah) speaks creation into existence[30]

Egyptian literature presents the means of creation of the universe in several different ways, but one means common with Genesis is the spoken word. In the Memphite Theology, Ptah brings forth Atum, the creator god, and then all the other gods through Atum by a divine command.[31] Though the spoken word or divine command is not the sole means of creation in Egyptian cosmogony, it is significant because it is early and widespread.[32]

Genesis 1	God is sovereign King of the universe
Egypt	The particular god presented as creator is also presented as the most significant god

The act of creation by divine command carries new theological significance that must be applied to Israel's God. In Egypt, the spoken word brings about reality, which is the role of the gods and the king. Whatever they said was supposed to come to pass:

In the created world, "Perception" and "Annunciation" are the means by which the forces of nature—the gods and the king—perceive what needs to be done and cause it to happen. Their function *par excellence*, however, is in the creation itself. The creator first perceives the world as a concept: "I became effective in my heart...I surveyed in my heart by myself" (Text 9, 12/18). He then gives reality to that perception through creative speech, "Annunciation, that spoke in the darkness" (CT VII 481g): I am the one who made what is and caused what was not to develop: when I spoke, Annunciation developed. (CT IV 145b–c)[33]

For the Egyptians, the presentation of a god as creator elevated that god to a ruling status. When a king spoke, his word happened. Or, to put it in reverse, if a word of command came to pass, such power revealed the speaker to be a ruler.[34] In Genesis, God's creative command demonstrates his rule. This culturally appropriate statement of God's rule would be most clear to Israel and all of Egypt at the time Israel leaves Egypt, because creation by divine command seems to be unique to the Egyptian materials, not being found in the Mesopotamian or Canaanite creation stories.[35] We will return to this in the purpose of the creation accounts.

Separation as Initial Acts of Creation

Genesis 1:3	Light created before the sun is in place
Egypt	Light is created before the sun rises in its place

In the Genesis account, the first thing God does on day 1 is call light into existence and then separate the light from the darkness (Gen. 1:3–4), thus establishing the *day*. The first main event in the Egyptian accounts is the separation of the waters to make an atmosphere. At first glance, this appears to be a difference between the Egyptian and Genesis accounts. In some Egyptian accounts, however, the god associated with the sun (Re) is the one that actually creates the atmosphere, and Atum (an alternative creator god) also becomes equated with the sun. In these accounts, then, the light does appear before the sun.[36] How can that be? From our perspective, there cannot be a sun if there is no atmosphere in which the sun can exist (and in their view, there is nothing but water everywhere). Yet, the Pyramid Texts relate the birth of Re in the dark, watery mass before there was sky.[37] The Egyptian perception is clearly very different from our modern perspective. They actually seem to have perceived of the god associated with the sun (and so light) without assuming the necessity of the sun itself. So, in fact, the Egyptians saw the separation of the waters as the first actual creative act, with the inception of light in the dark waters preceding that act, like the glow of the dawn before the actual rising of the sun.

A consistent riddle for biblical exegetes for centuries has been how to explain the existence of light on day 1 (Gen. 1:3–4) before the appearance of the sun on day 4 (Gen. 1:16–18). When we understand the Egyptian concept of light appearing in the dark water before the creation and the rising of the sun itself—which Israel would have known and probably accepted—we realize that when Israel heard Genesis 1:1–3, they would have envisioned a very different picture than our concept of some source of light out in an empty universe. We generally imagine a light in the sky with an empty cosmos already in place. We envision the earth, covered by water, rotating on its axis. But neither the Egyptian nor common Israelite perception (nor that of the rest of the ancient world) included any of these things. Instead, they perceived a light glowing in the midst of the dark waters that were still infinite and all-pervasive, not a light in or beyond an atmosphere, and not a sun. God does not choose to dispute this perception or explain any other options. He merely states that this light is his effortless creation, and, significantly, not a part of him. The separation of that light from the darkness would, additionally, accord well with their perception of the coming into being of "light" or, in Egyptian polytheism, the coming into existence of Re/Atum. The implications, however, are very significant. Light is not the creator but the created.

| Genesis 1:6–7 | God creates by separating the waters to create an atmosphere |
| Egypt | The god creates by separating the waters to create an atmosphere[38] |

In what seems to be the first main event of Egyptian creation accounts, Atum or Re (or Shu [atmosphere]) separates the waters to create a void (the "bubble" mentioned above) by his spoken word.[39] Morenz concludes that in the Egyptian accounts, separating is the primary means of creation.[40] Similarly in Genesis, not only is light separated from darkness (1:4), but the waters are separated from the waters to create the atmosphere (1:6–7), very much like the Egyptian accounts.

Again, the preconceptions of the Egyptians would be very different from our preconceptions. They viewed the sky as a void between themselves and a great ocean of water above it, with the lights of the sun, moon, and stars in between, sailing on the surface of that ocean. That sky ocean was held back by Shu (the atmosphere). In Genesis 1:6–7, the ocean of "waters above" are held back by a "firmament" (kjv) or "expanse" (esv), which Job portrays as "hard as a cast metal mirror" (37:18).[41] God merely refers to their perception of reality without explanation or contradiction.

| Genesis 1:9 | God creates by separating the land from the waters |
| Egypt | Initially in creation, the first little hillock of land (primordial mound) rises out of the water[42] |

In the Egyptian cosmogony, after the heavens are formed the waters recede, exposing the land. In some cases, a little mound of dirt known as the primordial mound on which Atum sat to create came into existence before the atmosphere. The main separation of the land and water occurred after the formation of the atmosphere. There is no record of a

The first land to appear in Egypt, the "primordial mound," provided the place for creation to begin and temples to be built. (Photo credit: John Soden)

god speaking this into existence; it just happens, apparently by volition of the gods (Geb [land] and Nut [waters]). The primary Egyptian god (Atum in Heliopolis or Ptah in Memphis) is associated with that little mound of dirt. Because creation started at that specific locale, the temples built there were supposedly built on that first primordial mound of dirt (as the center of that god's rule).[43] Similarly in Genesis, God gathers the waters, exposing the land (Gen. 1:9).

Creation of the Sun

| Genesis 1:14–18 | God creates the sun (day 4) after the light (day 1) |
| Egypt | The sun rises on the first day |

In the Egyptian accounts, the first sunrise is "the prime act of creation" for which the previous creative acts (atmosphere, sky, and so on, personalized as gods) form only a backdrop.[44] Everything has built up to this climax: it begins with the unlimited, dark, imperceptible water and the god of wind on the waters; then light emerges; then there is the separation of the waters to create an atmosphere; then the separation of land from water; and finally the sun is ready to rise triumphantly over the forces of chaos. The biblical account has a very similar order up to this point: it begins with desolation and emptiness with darkness over the deep; then God in Spirit (or "wind") hovers over the waters; then God speaks light into existence; he separates the waters to form an atmosphere; he separates land from water; then, after creating plants, God creates sun, moon, and stars.

However, in the biblical account, creation has not reached its climax. In Genesis 1:3 God creates the light (day 1), and in Genesis 1:14 he calls forth *the lights* by divine command, "making" the sun, moon, and stars, and then setting them in the heavens (1:16–17; all on day 4). The greater and lesser lights are merely "for signs and for seasons, and for days and years" (Gen. 1:14). They will rule, not like the supreme Egyptian sun deity, but only in a subservient capacity over day and night, and within the boundaries God has prescribed (Gen. 1:17–18). Creation is still waiting for its ruler and climax with the creation of mankind on day 6. While the order of events follows the order of the Egyptian accounts, the significance of the elements and the relationship to deity are dramatically distinct. Genesis allows no room for deity in the luminaries. They are merely servants of the Creator, doing his bidding.

Creation of Mankind

Genesis 1:26–28	God creates mankind in his image
Egypt	The gods create man in their image, formed out of clay

Another significant parallel between Genesis 1–2 and the Egyptian inscriptions appears in the Egyptian assertion that mankind was made in the likeness or image of the god (Re), formed by a potter (Khnum), and animated with the breath of a god (Re or Hekat).[45] For example, "The Instruction Addressed to King Merikare," speaking of Re, says that people are "his images, who came from his body" and so he takes care of them and disciplines them.[46] In other accounts, man is made by the tears of Atum's eye (the sun).[47]

In the Egyptian literature, the act of making man in the image of the god demonstrated the rule of the god over the man. For example, Re would guard and provide for mankind because people were his image, but he would also discipline them and kill the traitors among them to preserve mankind.[48] Being made in the image of the god also provides the basis for kingship and for Merikare's rule over the land (lines 139– 140), since he was the image and representative of the god.[49] Similarly, God's creation of man in his image certainly entails entrusting responsibility to mankind to represent him and rule for him.

God Rests

| Genesis 2:1–3 | After completing creation, God rested |
| Egypt | Ptah rested after completing his work of creation (Memphite Theology) |

In both cosmogonies, the creator rests in "satisfaction at the conclusion of a job well done."[50] The consistent judgment in Genesis 1 by God that what he made was "good" fits well the Egyptian concept of cosmic order.[51] According to the Memphite Theology, "So has Ptah come to rest after his making everything and every divine speech as well, having given birth to the gods, having made their towns, having founded their homes, having set the gods in their cult-places, having made sure their bread-offerings, having founded their shrines, having modelled their bodies to what contents them."[52]

Ptah rested when all the creating was done and all the gods were settled. God rests in Genesis 1 when all of creation is "good" and mankind is settled in charge of creation. While the two accounts are significantly different in worldview, they are significantly similar in the act of resting—not because of exhaustion but in recognition of and pleasure in a well-ordered creation.

Sequence of Events

Genesis 1:3–2:3	Out of desolate, empty, dark waters, God creates light, atmosphere, land, plants, the luminaries in the heavens, creatures, and man, and then he rests
Egypt	Out of unlimited, imperceptible, dark waters, the god creates himself (including light), atmosphere, land, and luminaries in the heavens (the sun rises), followed by plants, creatures, and man, and then he rests

As we have seen, the order of the Genesis creation account closely parallels the order of events in the Egyptian materials. In fact, the only clear difference is that in the Egyptian cosmogony the plants are created after the sun, whereas in the biblical account they appear on day 3, before the sun on day 4.[53] We will return to this difference in the next chapter.

The strong similarities between the accounts appear to draw the Israelites' perception back to a preconceived order of creation that Moses does not challenge.

Purpose of the Creation Accounts

Genesis 1–2	God as creator claims sovereignty over all creation and so all nations
Egypt	The creator god claims sovereign rule of state

Above, we noted the relationship between the divine command and the recognition or establishment of a ruler in creation. The primary

Egyptian creation accounts developed in the major cities of the kingdom—such as Memphis, Heliopolis, or Thebes—at various times, in order to exalt the main local god "to the rank of universal and officially recognized god of state, undergirding the city's claims to importance."[54] The account in Genesis 1 is concerned with much the same purpose. Genesis is not presenting a new local deity to Israel, but, as the introduction to the Pentateuch, it is calling for Israel's absolute allegiance to God, who claims absolute sovereign control. At the same time, the account demotes all the gods of Egypt and every other civilization with which Israel may have contact. Interestingly, the ten plagues were designed to reinforce this claim, not only for Israel but also for Egypt and the whole world.[55] God will be exalted among all nations as unique in power— there is none like him (Exod. 9:14–16; cf. 6:2–7; 7:3–5; 12:12; and see ch. 14 for an exposition of Yahweh's rule in the biblical perspective).

Summary

Put all the parallels between the creation accounts together, and we can see remarkable similarity (see figure 8).[56] In considering the correspondences between the two sets of creation accounts, "the magnitude of parallels cannot be by mere chance. We dare not call this situation a freak of antiquity."[57] There is clearly a correlation between the Egyptian material and the biblical account. We would expect this if Israel did indeed have a history in Egypt as the Old Testament claims. The significance is powerful. Understanding the biblical allusions to Egyptian mythology greatly enhances our understanding of the biblical text, including its theological perspective, and the worldview that Moses portrays with his account. The biblical similarities with and allusions to Egyptian creation accounts, however, ultimately serve to highlight the theological differences between Moses and the Egyptians. Genesis 1 challenges the theological suppositions Israel had learned in Egypt and would subsequently face with new neighbors.

Figure 8. Parallels Between Biblical and Egyptian Creation Accounts

Genesis 1:1–2:3	Egyptian Sources
Formless, void, darkness, deep (1:2)	Watery, unlimited, darkness, imperceptibility
"The Spirit of God was hovering over the face of the waters" (1:2)	The god of wind/breath on the waters
God creates by divine command (1:3, 6, 9, 11, 14–15, 20, 24)	Atum (or Ptah) speaks creation into existence
Light created before the sun is in place (1:3)	Light is created before the sun rises in its place
God creates by separating the waters to create an atmosphere (1:6–7)	The gods create by separating the waters to create an atmosphere
God creates by separating the land from the waters (1:9)	Initially in creation, the first little hillock of land (primordial mound) rises out of the water
God creates plants (1:11–12)	
God creates the sun (day 4) after the light (day 1) (1:14–18)	The sun rises on the first day
God creates fish, birds, and animal life (1:20–25)	The gods create plants, fish, birds, and animal life
God creates mankind in his image (1:26–28)	The gods create man in their image, formed out of clay
After completing creation, God rested (2:1–3)	Ptah rested after completing his work of creation (Memphite Theology)
Out of desolate, empty, dark waters, God creates light, atmosphere, land, plants, the luminaries in the heavens, creatures, and man, and then he rests (1:2–2:3)	Out of unlimited, imperceptible, dark waters, the god creates himself (including light), atmosphere, land, and luminaries in the heavens (the sun rises), followed by plants, creatures, and man; and then he rests
God as creator claims sovereignty over all creation and so all nations (1:2–2:3)	The creator god claims sovereign rule of state

Chapter Eight

GENESIS 1 DISTINGUISHED FROM THE EGYPTIAN CONTEXT

When you enter a different culture, how do you explain a new perspective to people who have a worldview and belief system very different from your own? In Acts 17, where Paul faces a polytheistic, idolatrous system in Athens and wants to tell them about the Lord Jesus, he begins to build a communication bridge by using the Athenians' own belief system. He tells them that their "unknown god" is really the sovereign creator of the universe, and that their own poets have unknowingly referred to him in their reflections (vv. 22–31). For the sake of argument, Paul assumes their poetic understanding that all men are God's "offspring," but this does not mean he would call all people "sons and daughters of God" in the same way he uses the phrase in Galatians where he says that believers in Christ are "children of God" (Gal. 3:26 NIV). He merely uses similar terminology to gain a hearing and lead the Athenian crowd to the true God.

Similarly, Moses starts with the Egyptian perception of the universe and then vigorously challenges their theology. By pointing out significant parallels with Egyptian thought in the previous chapter, we are not arguing that Moses merely borrowed his account of creation from Egypt. The magnitude of the distinctions discredits any such suggestion. We will see that in most cases, the biblical writer uses common motifs to demonstrate the stark differences in the Hebrew presentation of God. In other words, the considerable differences show that Genesis is not *copying* but *recasting* the events of creation in order to argue strongly for a different theology. While it is, therefore, a polemic (an argument disputing a particular theological understanding), it is not merely a polemic. Moses goes well beyond arguing against Egyptian deities and religious perceptions; he also presents a positive theology. To put it another way, Moses starts with what they know (or think they know), using a familiar vocabulary, in order to teach them what they need to know. He contextualizes the theology they must understand, beginning with aspects of their worldview that he can use as a frame both to build their understanding and to tear down their misunderstanding. Moses assumes a certain mind-set of the events or activities of creation, which were largely based on Israel's observations of the creation itself. He does not confront their cosmology any more than Jesus confronts the people's misperception that the sun rises (Matt. 5:45), but he confronts the false theology that accompanied the Egyptian perception of reality.

Let's consider the distinctions in theology between the two creation accounts.

Initial Conditions of Creation

Genesis 1:2	Formless, void, darkness, deep
Egypt	Watery, unlimited, darkness, imperceptibility

Moses begins at a place familiar to Israel and builds on their observations and common understanding. But he gives a very different meaning to their perspective by ascribing the creative activity to a transcendent God who is preexistent outside of the waters, not self-creating from within the waters. Genesis 1 focuses on the One who brought forth creation out of these conditions, thus presenting him as very different from the gods of the Egyptians. In Egypt, both the water (Nun) and everything that came out of it are deified. But Moses presents all of creation as nothing more than obedient subjects of God's command, without individual will or power. The God of Genesis 1 is outside of all creation and independent of it. He is entirely transcendent.

By beginning with the assumed precreation conditions that the Israelites would have understood, given their background in Egypt (specifically) and the ancient Near East (in general), the text clarifies the nature of God and his relationship to the creation. God does not comment on the accuracy of Israel's perception of the material world nor does he try to paint a comprehensive picture. Rather, he uses the Israelites' vocabulary for his statement of his role in his creation. As *The Dictionary of Biblical Imagery* states, "The images of the cosmos in the O[ld] T[estament] do not attempt to present an exhaustive explication of a complete cosmology. They are instead snippets, passing allusions to a common literary background of the ancient Semitic people. Only the literature of neighboring cultures presents a more coherent and complete presentation of this shared cosmological outlook."[1]

Genesis 1:2	"The Spirit of God was hovering over the face of the waters"
Egypt	The god of wind/breath on the waters[2]

Whether we understand Genesis 1:2 as referring to the breath or wind of God or to the Spirit of God (double entendre), its reference is not to a separate deity but to the presence and creative power of God himself. Even though involved and acting in creation, God is clearly still transcendent. He acts unilaterally by his own power. In addition, God does not create himself; he is preexistent. He is not identified with any beginning, and though he is recognized as acting in creation, he exists apart from creation.

Means of Creation

Genesis 1:3, 6, 9, 11, 14–15, 20, 24	God creates by divine command
Egypt	Atum (or Ptah) speaks creation into existence

In Genesis, God creates directly by divine command: "Let there be . . ." In the Memphite Theology, Ptah also creates by speaking, but it is the act of naming that appears to be central in the Egyptian account.[3] In Egypt, the act of naming produces the next tier of gods and, along with them, the elements of creation. In addition, the Egyptian concept of creating by command may have in mind the use of magic, calling on an outside power in creation. This use of magic distances Egyptian cosmogony dramatically from the biblical perception of God's absolute, powerful word of creation.[4] Israel's God creates effortlessly by his own power, calling all things into existence. He then names things after creating them, showing his sovereignty over creation. The elements he creates have no personality or divine essence. God alone is divine, and he is transcendent above his creation.

The Genesis account, which serves as the introduction to the history of mankind as well as to the Law, also reveals how God's spoken word creates, blesses, and continues to reveal his character in the lives of his people (Exod. 19:5–6; Ps. 19). In contrast to the Egyptian view of creation and its creator(s), Genesis presents one unique transcendent God over all of creation, with all creation bowing to his (ongoing) word.[5] In summary, while the method of creation is very similar, the Genesis creator is starkly different and his method is infused with new understanding.

Genesis 1	God is sovereign King of the universe
Egypt	The particular god being presented as creator is also being presented as the most significant god

Genesis does not merely elevate God over other gods; it presents God as transcendent and unique in *all* creation and as the *sole* claimant to deity. While Egypt and all other ancient Near Eastern peoples were polytheistic, Israel alone was monotheistic. While all other gods were aspects of creation, Israel's God alone was outside of creation and in complete control of all creation. Genesis 1 proclaims that God alone is Creator, the Sovereign of everything!

Separation as Initial Acts of Creating

| Genesis 1:3 | Light is created before the sun is in place |
| Egypt | Light is created before the sun rises in its place |

While God does not correct some ancient expressions of how the world functions, he does illuminate ancient theological misconceptions. He makes it clear that the created light is not a supreme god. It is neither the self-creation nor aura of a great deity, but the effortless creation of the only deity. The light itself is not an attribute or part of God, but a part of the elements under God's supreme control, something he adds to creation.

> While the Egyptian creator-god Rê/Rê-Atum came into existence at this point, the God of Israel is preexistent and the supernatural light was not a manifestation of His self-creation, but of the power of His command, "Let there be light!" The appearance of this motif in Genesis, far from marking the moment of the self-generation of God, is a case of the Hebrew author indulging in a bit of one-upmanship. Yahweh is superior to Rê/Rê-Atum, Egypt's god of light.[6]

| Genesis 1:6–7 | God creates by separating the waters to create an atmosphere |

Egypt	The gods create by separating the waters to create an atmosphere

Genesis does not try to correct a perception of reality that assumes a watery mass above the vault of the sky. God does not reveal the astronomical realities of outer space to a people schooled in Egyptian cosmology. Instead Genesis 1 reveals a transcendent God who made the ordered universe, providing an ordered place for his creatures to inhabit.

The biblical text clearly and consistently separates the theology of Israel from the surrounding peoples, particularly Egypt. None of the created elements are personal deities with independent powers, nor are they struggling with God and trying to undo creation. They are merely the subservient effects of his creative word. Yahweh is completely sovereign over all aspects of his creation.

Genesis 1:9	God creates by separating the land from the waters
Egypt	Initially in creation, the first little hillock of land (primordial mound) rises out of the water

While the appearance of the land in Genesis 1 is similar in order and action to Egyptian accounts, it has a very different theological impact. In the Egyptian cosmogony, the first little hill of land that appears, the primordial mound, represents the place with premier religious significance and the beginning of all life. As such, it was associated with Atum or Ptah or other chief gods. The Egyptians conceived of this mound of earth as the place to build temples (for many deities) where the gods would be enthroned on the top of the mound and where the king would sit as ruler of the world.[7] The biblical account, however, presents the creation of land as just another act of God's creation to make his desolate and empty earth productive and inhabited—a step in the preparation of the earth as a fit place for his creation of man. The biblical account

The "first pylon," a monumental gateway to the temple of Amun-Re in Karnak, Egypt. (Photo credit: James Hoffmeier)

does not claim that one particular place is where the world originated or where God or man is to be enthroned to demonstrate sovereignty. Instead it points to the sovereign claim of God to all the earth, not only to a small original hillock.

Creation of the Sun

Genesis 1:14–18	God creates the sun (day 4) after the light (day 1)
Egypt	The sun rises on the first day

In the biblical account the sun is far different from Re, the creative force and prime mover of Egyptian creation. God does not name it, because that would remind Israel of a perceived deity, since in ancient Near Eastern cultures the name of the sun was used for a deity. Instead Genesis dishonors it—the word *sun* doesn't even appear—and merely calls it the "greater light," highlighting its submission to the complete verbal control of God. God has placed it in the heavens for a purpose, but it is not the main actor on creation's stage. Instead the sun is merely the biggest of the lights in the sky, which God ordains for his purpose: to rule over the day, separate light from darkness, give light to the earth, and be for signs and seasons, days and years.

Sunrise is no longer the prime event of creation. The prime event is reserved for the creation of man on day 6. The placement of the sun in the account (on day 4) seems to signal a new thrust of creation: days 4–6 mirror and complement days 1–3 and build to the climax of mankind. The climax of biblical creation will be mankind as the image of God, not the sun as an embodiment of a god (such as Re, Atum, or Amun).

Creation of Mankind

Genesis 1:26–28	God creates mankind in his image
Egypt	The gods create man in their image, formed out of clay

The biblical account emphasizes that man having been created in the image of God is the basis for mankind to represent God and to rule over creation. Genesis 1 presents male and female as fully capable, blessed by God, and not marred or tainted by anything that would keep them from accomplishing their role ("very good").

The biblical account also does not assign any particular individual (Pharaoh), in his role as the visible image of the god, to be king over others; rather, it seems to envision mankind as representative of God and ruling with him over creation. All mankind, not just one king (as in Egypt), are intermediaries between God and creation, representing and ruling for God in his image.

God Rests

Genesis 2:1–3	After completing the work, God rested

| Egypt | Ptah rested after completing his work of creation (Memphite Theology) |

Genesis presents God resting on the seventh day, blessing and sanctifying that day to show his completion of and satisfaction with creation and his sole authority over it. The Egyptian cosmogony presents Ptah resting in a job well done, while all of the other gods come to him in contentment and satisfaction at his provision for them.[8] Ptah completed all of creation in one day, not seven. Ptah did not bless a day or sanctify it. In fact, every day reenacts Ptah's creation.

By contrast, for Israel, creation is not reenacted daily. It was done once with a goal in mind. The cyclical view from Egypt repeated as "the first occasion," which showed that the daily rising of the sun reenacted creation, becomes "in the beginning," which portrays creation as an initial act with a goal in mind. History thus becomes linear and goal oriented, rather than cyclical and endlessly repetitious. Israel was instructed to rest with their God on the seventh day in celebration of and satisfaction with God's work. The seventh day became for Israel a commitment to God as Lord in imitation and dependence.[9]

Sequence of Events

| Genesis 1:3–2:3 | Out of desolate, empty, dark waters, God creates light, atmosphere, land, plants, sun in the heavens, creatures, man in seven days, and then he rests |
| Egypt | Out of unlimited, imperceptible, dark waters, the god creates himself (including light), atmosphere, land, and luminaries in the heavens (the sun rises), followed by plants, creatures, and man, and then he rests |

We have noted how the order of events is dramatically similar in the creation accounts. The differences, however, are theologically significant and present a unique view of the function of creation and the role of the creator.[10]

First, the appearance of the sun as the initial and main event in Egyptian theology is challenged in Genesis 1, which holds back the appearance of the sun until day 4. The issue is not so much the change in order (it is still the same, except for the appearance of plant life). Rather the use of the "week" in creation instead of a single day delays the event of the sunrise from the first morning to the fourth day. The sun is no longer the dominant force or king over the gods (even though it was to "rule the day"; Gen. 1:16). The sun is just another of God's submissive creations, doing his bidding and serving his will. The resulting picture dramatically downplays the sun, Egypt's main actor. Instead, God clearly shines as the sovereign and transcendent ruler of creation. The climax becomes the creation of mankind as God's representative.

Second, the change in the order of events embeds a theological point in the literary form by focusing attention on the parallels between days 3 and 6. Each day has two creative events, climaxing with plants and people, respectively. Futato points out the parallel and dual focus on plants and people between the accounts of Genesis 1 and 2, which leads him to conclude theologically that Israel needed to recognize God, rather than Baal, as the giver of vegetation and life.[11] Vegetation will become vital to the issue for man in the succeeding story, in which man takes center stage and falls in Genesis 2–3. The two main aspects of the creation that present the conflict in the second section of Genesis (especially chapters 2–3) are then highlighted. Plants form the occasion for man's temptation to rebel against his beneficent creator.

The very obvious difference in the two presentations of creation is that the Egyptian creation occurs all in one day; there is no concept of successive days of creation, much less of seven days in particular. This third distinction is also theologically significant. For Egypt, the creation event was reenacted in their experience *every day*. The time between evening and morning was a struggle as the sun battled darkness and chaos, but ultimately "the sun-god emerge[d] every morning from the primeval ocean Nun and by his daily journey ensure[d] order in the cosmos."[12] The theology of victory over chaos in creation also shows up in Egypt's view of history in the repetition of the creation event, as the king drives chaos out of the land (militarily) and restores order.[13]

The creation of the world in seven successive days in Genesis 1 militates strongly against such a worldview. Creation is not reenacted each day, nor does each day represent a struggle between the gods to maintain order. Rather, the seven "days" of creation prepared Israel to experience and, in a tangible way, to celebrate the rule of God over creation by participating in his rest each week in the Sabbath observance (Exod. 20:8–11; 31:12–17). In Exodus 31, the Sabbath is a "sign" to Israel that reminded them of their relationship with God (via the covenant). Celebrating the Sabbath after six days of work demonstrated that Israel shared in God's work and in his rest and that they had submitted to the creator of the universe. For Israel, days never indicated uncertainty about the future or questions about God's rule and ultimate victory. There was no ongoing celestial struggle, only the daily and weekly requirement to trust and submit to the giver of life and blessing—to declare allegiance to the one who rules all things.

There is another obvious exegetical detail that is clearly significant, but that has been difficult to pinpoint. With each day, except the seventh, the text repeats the refrain that "there was evening and there was morning," and then it numbers the day. This refrain occurs at the end of the first six days as a transition to the next. While we have already suggested that the missing refrain in day 7 suggests a nonliteral understanding of the week, there may also be another reason for stating it in each of the first six days beyond merely marking the time. Several issues may apply here.

In Egyptian mythology, the sun god descends into the dark unordered realm of chaos (the primeval ocean) each succeeding night after creation and fights the serpent Apophis or Apepi. In repelling Apophis, the sun rises victoriously the next morning, reenacting creation anew

In Egyptian mythology, the sun god descends into the dark, unordered realm of chaos (the primeval ocean) each succeeding night after creation and fights the serpent Apophis. (Photo credit: Frederick J. Mabie)

each day and assuring another day of order and life.[14] "In this way each day brings both a confirmation of the order established at the first time and also a forcible reconquest of it."[15] In fact, it was precisely at sunset and at dawn that the dragon-snake Apepi would attack the boat of the sun as it was leaving the sky and entering the Duat, just before rising again the next day.[16] Perhaps this belief accounts for the benign repetition of the phrase, "there was evening and there was morning, day x" after days 1–6 (Gen. 1:5, 8, 13, 19, 23, 31).

The Genesis account is dramatically different. God does not maintain creation through an ongoing battle against chaos. Instead, God decisively reframed the desolation and darkness of creation into a good, life-sustaining environment. The transition between days shows no struggle, but instead exhibits a sequential building of order, effortlessly moving from day to day, from one to seven, without any reference to a time lapse. Genesis merely mentions the crucial times of evening and morning rhythmically passing, while in Egypt, the passage of time foreboded warfare with chaos. By contrast, Israel's God easily manages time, and any sense of danger vanishes en route to his glorious and ordered rest. Such a picture directly opposes the Egyptian concept of "the cycle of life and human destiny, determined by the daily drama of sunset and sunrise."[17]

When we get to day 7 in Genesis, there is not even a mention of evening and morning, as if there is no longer a hint of darkness and chaos in God's very good creation. In fact, Hebrews 4:1–4 indicates the theological significance of this by recognizing that day 7 was unending, just as God's rest and our ultimate rest with him are unending. Such an ongoing rest directly contrasts the prevailing Egyptian theology of the sun's struggle for life, rule, and daily order.

The significance of the lack of the article ("the") on the first five days of creation may also be understood in this light. When Genesis 1:5 presents the first creative period as "one day" instead of "the first day," it may be intentionally rejecting the Egyptian notion of seeing creation reenacted each day. The Egyptians viewed creation as "the first time," and it was subsequently repeated every day.[18] As mentioned above, this view is directly contradicted by the "in the beginning" of Genesis 1. The Hebrew text then takes pains to dispute the daily repetition of creation, instead spreading it out over multiple days: "one day," "a second day," and so on. Each new day is independent of the power of the sun or the deities of Egypt. The significance of the week is not in its chronology of six successive twenty-four-hour days but in its distancing of Israel's theology from that of the Egyptians. Genesis presents the completion of creation as a process of days to be imitated and enjoyed, rather than as an initial pattern that is repeated in violent uncertainty until creation finally dissolves back into the dark watery chaos in some distant future.

Creation cannot be reenacted each day. It is only recognized (not repeated) in the workweek. God established a new paradigm for understanding his sovereign control of all creation and for demonstrating submission and allegiance to his rule. The Israelites were to celebrate their creator's sovereign establishment of order and blessing, to rule over the creation, and to reflect him to the world on the seventh day, a blessed and sanctified rest that celebrated and illustrated God's satisfying of their needs (Exod. 19:5–6; 31:12–17).

Purpose of the Creation Accounts

Genesis 1–2	God as creator claims sovereignty over all creation and so all nations
Egypt	The creator god claims sovereign rule of state

The biblical claims for God, as introduced by the creation narratives, are not that he is one supreme god over the other gods. Instead, Genesis argues for a unique and sole claimant to supremacy over all of creation. The biblical account does not admit to any other deities in creation or above creation. As stated earlier,[19] this theology of creation gives God the right to rule his creation at his sole discretion, including granting land to Israel (Gen. 14:19, 22 with 15:17–20; Jer. 27:5; Ps. 115:15–16; Dan. 4:17, 25, 32) and dealing with all other nations, including Egypt, as he chooses. He can therefore bring judgment against all the gods of Egypt (Exod. 12:12).

Tsumura aptly summarizes, "… in the Old Testament theology, when Yahweh-Elohim is represented as the creator of heaven and earth (e.g., Gen.1:1; 14:22), the author is saying not only that he is incomparable in relation to other gods but also that, as the actual creator, he is the only god who can truly be called a god; that is, he is God."[20]

Summary

Moses does not directly dispute the events of creation, but he uses common Egyptian perceptions of creation to present a radically different and unique understanding of God and his relationship to man in his world. To summarize these distinctions:

1. *God in Genesis exists independently of creation and is not created or self-created.* God is completely distinct from creation and outside

of creation. There is no sense in which creation is part of God or God is equated with creation.

2. *God alone transcends creation.* Moses' God, Israel's God, exercises absolute, effortless power in his creation.

3. *God is sovereign over all creation.* In Genesis, all of creation answers to the word of Yahweh. He does not require any magic or outside power but commands total control with his own power.

4. *God alone is deity.* None of creation has a will of its own or can impact history as the Egyptians perceived of their deities. The omission of names for the key players in the Egyptian cosmology (the greater light and lesser light, for example) highlights the de-personalization of the cosmos and its submission to the will of the creator. Not only is there no account of the creation of gods, there is the clear implication that no gods are created.

5. *Mankind has great significance and value as God's image.* Mankind replaces the sun as the central focus of creation and the climax of that creation. All of creation prepares for the existence of mankind, the ruling representative and lead worshiper of God on earth. The elements of creation all provide benefit to man, not man to the elements of creation (as gods).

6. *Israel was to celebrate the rule of God in their lives by imitating their Creator in work and rest each week.* In their marking of time and their struggle to survive for six days each week (the curse of the fall, Gen. 3:18–19), they find rest in submission to God's rule and they experience his provision by faith (Sabbath rest). This weekly respite presents a dramatic shift from the daily conquest of the sun god over chaos, his rebirth each morning, and the daily grind of uncertainty in each Egyptian day. Each day in Egypt was a self-contained creation account with no certainty of the next. Israel, however, could live in hope of God as the singular and sovereign Creator who does not struggle to survive. Instead, he has absolute reign over creation, a sovereignty that gave them confidence in the future. The week gave them an ongoing object lesson, not

of creation and struggle but of their tie to their creator and their confidence for blessing in his work on their behalf.

As a narrative, the creation account presents a compelling and unique picture of Israel's Yahweh Elohim, which will be backed up by the mighty wonders in the Exodus. It provides the foundation for Israel's covenant, giving their purpose and future within all of God's creation: "You yourselves have seen what I did to the Egyptians, and how I bore you on eagles' wings and brought you to myself. Now therefore, if you will indeed obey my voice and keep my covenant, you shall be my treasured possession among all peoples, for all the earth is mine; and you shall be to me a kingdom of priests and a holy nation" (Exod. 19:4–6).

Chapter Nine

GENESIS 1 COMPARED WITH THE MESOPOTAMIAN CONTEXT

E gypt was not the only influence on Israel's understanding of creation. The ancient Near East was not a collection of completely isolated nations; religious myths and beliefs flowed freely between peoples from different backgrounds, much as philosophy is exchanged between higher education communities in the United States today. If Egypt was a university setting on the west coast, Mesopotamia was such a setting in the east (though only about eight hundred miles as the crow flies from Egypt). Mesopotamia was Abraham's ancestral home, the source of his religious indoctrination until God (Yahweh) called him to journey to the land of Canaan.

Yet the descendants of Abraham were hundreds of years removed from his ancestral home. Did Mesopotamia still have an influence on their worldview? Did the beliefs of the Mesopotamian cosmogony transcend nationality in the ancient world so that an understanding of them can provide a broader framework for God's earliest theology lessons for Israel? The proximity between Mesopotamia and Egypt was close enough and the influence broad enough that we can be sure Mesopotamian theology had an impact across the ancient world. A parallel to this reality is the way that Hinduism has influenced Western society through the New Age movement.

In this chapter we will compare Mesopotamian creation accounts to determine how closely they parallel Genesis 1. As with the Egyptian accounts, there are many references to creation and initial conditions in Mesopotamian texts that fall short of an ordered account of all of creation. These fragmentary references appear in god lists, narrative texts, incantations, rites, temple dedications, prayers, disputations, and longer narratives built around the exaltation of a god or explanation of human society and mortality.[1] Only two texts provide creation accounts of significant length. The longer account, the Epic of Creation (or *Enuma Elish*[2]), includes the story of the creation of the universe and man. It was written as a defense of the god Marduk's claim to be sovereign over all the gods. The second account, the Epic of Atrahasis, is the earliest orderly relating of the beginnings of mankind and its near extinction by the gods. It does not include the creation of the universe, but it includes the creation of mankind and parallels Genesis 2–11 in general structure, following the creation of man with the story of a flood as the gods try to destroy mankind.

Beginnings According to Mesopotamia
Enuma Elish

Enuma Elish begins with the primordial waters, Tiamat (salt water, the deep) and Apsu (fresh water). A third god, Mummu (possibly the mist) appears as vizier to Apsu. Nothing was yet created (there is no heaven or netherworld). The fresh and salt water commingled and produced the first generation of the gods. A problem that Tiamat and Apsu had not foreseen, however, was that their children would make so much noise that Apsu could not sleep. The sleep-deprived father got upset and decided to destroy their children, but one of the children, Ea (god of rivers and streams), heard about the plan, put Apsu to sleep with his magic, and killed him. Ea then built his own temple and rested there. He fathered offspring of his own, beginning with Marduk, the god of storm. Marduk, greater than all the other gods, played with the winds

The Mesopotamian creation account, *Enuma Elish*, was recorded on clay tablets. (Photo credit: Baker Photo Archive)

he was given, roiling up the waters of Tiamat and keeping the older gods awake.

Then the irritated gods wanted to kill Marduk and the gods that were with him. Tiamat set forth her own candidate to be king of the gods—Qingu—and went to war against Anshar, the old king of the gods. Marduk's father and grandfather were unable to stand against her. Marduk, invited to join the fight against Tiamat, agreed on the condition that he would be made the greatest of the gods. The other gods agreed and gave him the ability to create and destroy by divine command. Marduk then warred against Tiamat, and in single combat he slew her and divided her body into two parts—half of which he used to

Figure 9. Gods of Mesopotamia	
Anshar	• the sky god from the second generation of gods (son of Tiamat and Apsu) • the old king of the gods
Anu	• a son of Anshar • also the sky god and king of the gods
Apsu	• the deified underground waters (fresh waters) • consort of Tiamat, with whom he created the second generation of gods
Ea	• god of rivers and streams
Enki	• god of water and wisdom • also called Ea
Enlil	• god of air and weather • in some myths he helped create humans
Marduk	• god of the storm • son of Ea • heir of Anu • became head of the pantheon and assumed the qualities of Ea and Enlil
Mummu	• god of the mist • vizier for Apsu
Nanna (Sin)	• moon god and god of wisdom • main worship centers were in Ur and Haran of Abraham fame.
Qingu/Kingu	• son of Tiamat (and her consort after the murder of Apsu) • attempted to be king of the gods • his blood was used to make mankind
Shamash	• sun god associated with law and justice • the son of Nanna, the moon god
Sin	*see* Nanna
Tiamat	• the deified waters of the sea (salt waters) • consort of Apsu until he was murdered.

make heaven, and half of which he used for the waters of the lands and netherworld. He founded the temples for his fathers and established the stars, the moon, and sun for years and months and signs. The gods confirmed Marduk as absolute king, and he built his own temple to establish his kingship.

Since the other gods proclaimed his majesty, Marduk decided to ease their burden by creating man to do their work so they could rest. He condemned Qingu as the perpetrator of the war, put him to death, and let Ea use his blood to create man. The other gods then took their places in the creation and reaffirmed Marduk as king of all. (See, in summary, figure 9.)

Atrahasis

According to *Atrahasis*, named after the very wise man and hero who survived the great flood and saved mankind from destruction, mankind was created to relieve the working gods. The lower gods had to do all the work for the higher gods. Feeling overworked, they rebelled. When the higher gods realized the work was too demanding for them to do themselves, they created mankind to their work instead. In order to create mankind, they killed one god and mixed his flesh and blood with clay to form a man; this gave mankind the spirit of the god. Mankind then took over the work of caring for the gods.

Problems arose when mankind multiplied. The people were too noisy and disturbed the gods, so the gods decided to reduce the population by disease and starvation. Enki, the god of wisdom (later known as Ea), intervened by advising Atrahasis how to save the human race. He advised Atrahasis to get the people to pray to the god of disease instead of to their normal gods so that he would relent from the calamity. It worked, but then the noise again bothered Enlil who decreed drought and famine. Enki again saved mankind with the same advice to worship the god of the storm and by providing fish. Finally, when man's noise became intolerable again, Enlil decided to destroy mankind with a flood. Enki again intervened and advised Atrahasis to build a boat. The flood destroyed most people, but then the gods got hungry and thirsty because there was no one to take care of them. When they realized Atrahasis had survived, they were glad, but they agreed to limit the repopulation of the people by limiting who could reproduce.

Initial Considerations of Beginnings According to Mesopotamia

Aside from *Enuma Elish* and *Atrahasis*, many other texts briefly

Mesopotamians pictured the universe with six different layers, including three heavens and three levels of earth. (Rebekah Fry)

reference creation and credit other gods for the basic aspects of creation.[3] None of these texts, however, was written simply to express a theology of creation. Rather, each account had a greater purpose. In the case of *Enuma Elish*, the purpose was to provide the rationale for the rule and coronation of Marduk as king over the gods. *Atrahasis* focuses on the creation of people to take care of the gods and explains mankind's mortality.

Some accounts that only touch on creation highlight the functions of the temple, where the gods received their due, and the king's role in the organization and orderliness of the temple, in order to show that mankind's purpose was to care for the gods.[4] Some texts that reference creation introduce incantations that appear to try to flatter the gods into providing health or some other benefit. While all the accounts assume a very different worldview and perspective on creation (see chapter 10), they also have many similarities with the Genesis 1 account. In this chapter, we will consider these similarities.

Initial Conditions of Creation

Genesis 1:2	Desolate, empty, darkness, deep
Mesopotamia	Infinite (?) watery chaos, (darkness?)

As with Genesis 1 and the Egyptian accounts, the Mesopotamian beginnings consistently start with a preexisting watery mass.[5] Most commonly, as in *Enuma Elish*, the watery mass is actually a god in battle against the creator, but sometimes the water is merely a passive sea with no picture of combat.[6]

The state of darkness with the water before creation may be implied in the Mesopotamian accounts, but is not clearly stated.[7] What is clear, however, is that a chaotic mass of water with no apparent beginning already existed before the creation of the gods or the universe. When we compare what we saw in the Egyptian accounts, we realize that a preexisting watery mass was a common belief.

Means of Creation

Genesis 1:3, 6–7, 9, 11, 14–16, 20, 24–26, 31; 2:2–3	God creates by divine command and "making"
Mesopotamia	Marduk destroys and restores a constellation with his word; creation is done by crafting

While Marduk is able to destroy and restore a constellation by the power of his word and thus exhibit his divine supremacy,[8] his command is not used to create the universe. Instead, in the Mesopotamian accounts the creator gods always form the cosmos and its elements as a man would create—by physical work. For example, in *Enuma Elish* Marduk divides Tiamat to be used for the heavens above and waters below,[9] but in the Eridu Genesis, the waters were already there and Marduk forms the land by creating dirt and pouring it on a raft on top of the waters.[10] *Enuma Elish* does not talk about the land and the Eridu Genesis does not state how the dirt was created.

In Genesis 1, while creation is clearly the general result of divine command, the biblical text states seven times that God "made" elements of his creation (the expanse [1:7], the luminaries [1:16], the beasts [1:25], man [1:26], everything [1:31; 2:2–3]). And, of course, Genesis 2:7 refers to God forming man from "the dust of the ground," using a Hebrew term that could refer to a potter or metalworker (cf. Isa. 44:9, 10, 12).

Light Before Luminaries

Genesis 1:3–5, 14–18	God creates light on day 1 before the luminaries on day 4
Mesopotamia	Light, day, and night exist before the luminaries are created

In both the biblical and Mesopotamian accounts, day and night exist before the luminaries are created. In *Enuma Elish*, the problem Apsu had with the noise of the created gods was not being able to sleep at night. His vizier, Mummu, counseled him to put an end to the younger gods because, "By day you should have rest, at night you should sleep."[11] The account implies that there is alternating light and dark (that is, days) even without a sun, just as in the first three days of Genesis, there was light and dark before the creation of the sun on day 4.

In addition, Marduk is called "The son, the sun, the sunlight of the gods."[12] Horowitz concludes that "the heavens are conceived to have had their own glow, irrespective of the presence of luminaries."[13] All of this is before the creation of the cosmos and demonstrates a common belief that light could and did exist before and apart from the sun.

Separation as the Initial Act of Creation

Genesis 1:6–8	God creates by separating the waters. to create an atmosphere
Mesopotamia	The gods create by separating the waters to create an atmosphere

Many scholars have compared God's separation of the waters in Genesis 1 to the description in *Enuma Elish* of Marduk defeating and dividing Tiamat (the primordial waters) into heaven and the netherworld. In Genesis 1:2, 6, God separates the deep (*tehom*) into the waters above and the waters below the expanse.[14] In the Sumerian account, Enlil (god of air) separates the waters of heaven and earth.[15] As with other comparisons, there are basic similarities in the separation of the waters above and below the atmosphere.

These similarities may simply demonstrate that there was a basic conception of the beginnings of the universe that consistently pervaded the ancient Near East. The notion began with the waters and bringing creation out of them, a concept that God chose not to dispute in Genesis 1. Just as the preexistence of a watery mass seems to be common to nearly all creation accounts from ancient civilizations, so also the beginning of creation with a separation of this water by a firmament or atmosphere to hold them apart seems to be a common feature.[16]

Creation of Sun, Moon, and Stars (and Light)

Genesis 1:14–18	God creates sun, moon, and stars for signs, seasons, days, and years, and to give light
Mesopotamia	The gods create sun, moon, and stars for signs, seasons, days, and years, and to give light

Enuma Elish pictures in detail Marduk creating the stars to mark the years, the moon to mark the months, and all the heavenly bodies to provide signs.[17] One minor account depicts Anu, Enlil, and Ea establishing the moon to create the month, to be a sign of heaven and earth, and to give light to the earth. Another minor account shows Anu, Enlil, and Ea establishing the sun in the midst of the heaven and earth.[18]

By comparison, Genesis 1:14–18 highlights the same purposes for the moon and for the giving of light. *Enuma Elish*, however, presents the sun last and does not state a purpose for the sun. Perhaps the purpose is assumed, but the biblical order of the elements is closer to the Egyptian presentation than to the Mesopotamian account.

Creation of Mankind

Genesis 2:7	God formed man from the dust and breathed into him the breath of life
Mesopotamia	The gods formed man from clay (and blood of a god) to do their work

In Mesopotamian accounts, mankind is generally represented as being formed out of the blood of a god mixed with clay.[19] In some accounts, however, people sprout like plants from the ground or are formed in molds.[20] The similarity in creation is not nearly as close to the biblical account as in the Egyptian material.

While there is some parallel in the formation of man, the purpose of man in Mesopotamia is very different. There is no mention of man as the image of the gods, nor of the breath of life. The idea of the blood of a god implies a divine source of life and perhaps an enduring uniqueness to the character of mankind, but man is not created to represent the gods or to rule. In *Enuma Elish*, man is created to do the work the gods are tired of doing: man is merely a servant to care for the gods.

God Rests

Genesis 2:1–3	God rests on the seventh day
Mesopotamia	The gods rest after man is created, and gods typically rest in temples they build

There is a basic correspondence between the Mesopotamian accounts and the Genesis 1 account in the occurrence of rest after creation. The culminating event in *Enuma Elish* is the coronation of Marduk and the building of his temple, the place where he rests.[21] Parallel to this Mesopotamian expectation that a god rests in his temple, we might expect God's rest (day 7) to be in *his* temple.

Building on this ancient Near Eastern concept of a god resting in a temple, John Walton argues that Genesis 1 presents the inauguration of Yahweh's cosmic temple. As the Mesopotamian god builds and rests in his temple in *Enuma Elish*, so Yahweh builds and rests in his temple in Genesis 1:1–2:3.[22] The seven days of creation establish the functions of the universe in order to inaugurate all of creation as the temple of God.[23] The Scripture elsewhere picturesquely relates all of creation to God's temple (Isa. 66:1; Ps. 11:4) and recognizes the temple as God's resting place (2 Chron. 6:41–42; Ps. 132:7–8). While we may assume this kind of imagery in Genesis 1, the text nonetheless does not clearly present an inauguration of a cosmic temple.

Sequence of Events

Genesis 1:3–2:3	Out of desolate, empty, dark waters, God creates light, atmosphere, land, the luminaries in the heavens, creatures, and man, and then he rests
Mesopotamia	From primeval dark chaos the gods create atmosphere, land, luminaries in the heavens, creatures, and man, and then they rest[24]

None of the Mesopotamian accounts has all of the events of the Genesis 1 account, so the reconstruction is not quite the same as the biblical account. The accounts generally follow the same sequence up to day 4: water pervades everything; light exists; water is separated to provide atmosphere and netherworld; land is made; sun, moon, and stars are created. These similarities are significant, perhaps demonstrating a similar understanding of creation across the ancient world.

However, the order of the creation of man and animals is not clear in the available accounts from Mesopotamia. The Chaldean cosmogony seems to put man first followed by some beasts, the plants, and more animals (similar to Gen. 2), while "The Creation of the Living Creatures" mentions the animals before man (perhaps like Gen. 1).[25] The Mesopotamian accounts, then, do not as clearly parallel Genesis 1 as the Egyptian accounts.

Purpose of the Creation Accounts

Genesis 1:2–2:3	God as creator claims sovereignty over all creation and so over all nations
Mesopotamia	Presentation of the gods' authority over their realms of creating

In Mesopotamia, the creation accounts intend to demonstrate the sovereignty and authority of a particular god. *Enuma Elish*, for example (along with the Chaldean cosmogony), forms the backdrop to Marduk's coronation and kingship, followed by the building of his temple. The minor cosmogonies may call on a god to act by reminding him of his authority over a realm based on his creation of it: because he created it, he should act to maintain its created purpose or assigned destiny.[26]

As with *Enuma Elish* and its apology for Marduk as the king of the gods, the biblical account presents the sovereign nature and authority of God over his creation. Genesis 1 calls Israel to absolute allegiance to their God, the sole claimant to their loyalty.

Summary

The Mesopotamian literature does not have as many parallels with Genesis 1 as the Egyptian materials, nor are they as close in comparison (see figure 10). When the Babylonian (Mesopotamian) creation

Figure 10. Parallels Between Biblical, Egyptian, and Mesopotamian Creation Accounts

Genesis 1:1–2:3	Egyptian accounts	Mesopotamian accounts
Formless, void, darkness, deep (1:2)	Watery, unlimited, darkness, imperceptibility	Infinite (?) watery chaos, (darkness?)
"The Spirit of God was hovering over the face of the waters" (1:2)	The god of wind/breath on the waters	
God creates by divine command (1:3, 6, 9, 11, 14–15, 20, 24)	Atum (or Ptah) speaks creation into existence	Marduk destroys and restores a constellation with his word; creation is done by crafting
Light is created before the sun is in place (1:3)	Light is created before the sun rises in its place	Light, day, and night exist before the luminaries are created
God creates by separating the waters to create an atmosphere (1:6–7)	The gods create by separating the waters to create an atmosphere	The gods create by separating the waters to create an atmosphere
God creates by separating the land from the waters (1:9)	Initially in creation, the first little hillock of land (primordial mound) rises out of the water	
God creates plants (1:11–12)		
God creates the sun, moon, and stars for signs, seasons, days, and years, and to give light (day 4) after the light (day 1) (1:14–18)	The sun rises on the first day	The gods create sun, moon, and stars for signs, seasons, days, and years, and to give light
God creates fish, birds, and animal life (1:20–25)	The gods create plants, fish, birds, and animal life	
God creates mankind in his image (1:26–28)	The gods create man in their image, formed out of clay	The gods formed man from clay (and blood of a god) to do their work
After completing creation, God rests (2:1–3)	Ptah rested after completing his work of creation (Memphite Theology)	The gods rest after man is created, and gods typically rest in temples they build

Continued

	Figure 10 continued	
Genesis 1:1–2:3	**Egyptian accounts**	**Mesopotamian accounts**
Out of desolate, empty, dark waters, God creates light, atmosphere, land, plants, the luminaries in the heavens, creatures, and man, and then he rests (1:2–2:3)	Out of unlimited, imperceptible, dark waters, the god creates himself (including light), atmosphere, land, and luminaries in the heavens (the sun rises), followed by plants, creatures, and man, and then he rests	From primeval waters the gods create atmosphere, land, luminaries in the heavens, creatures, and man, and then they rest
God as Creator claims sovereignty over all creation and so over all nations (1:2–2:3)	The creator god claims sovereign rule of state	The gods claim authority over their realm of creating

accounts were first discovered, many scholars assumed that the Genesis account borrowed from them. Some scholars still assume direct dependence of Genesis on the Mesopotamian accounts, but many scholars have increasingly recognized the significant differences and have rejected the dependence of Moses in any direct way upon the Babylonian material.[27] The similarities of the Mesopotamian accounts to Genesis 1 seem to be more in broad strokes and major themes, while closer parallels exist with the Egyptian accounts—a situation we might expect given the biblical claim that Israel spent four hundred years in Egypt. The creation account in Genesis 1 suggests that Moses used common ideas regarding the elements of creation in the ancient Near East, from both Mesopotamia and Egypt. As with the Egyptian creation accounts, the differences between Genesis 1 and the Mesopotamian accounts are also stark and significant. To these specific differences we now turn.

Chapter Ten

GENESIS 1 DISTINGUISHED FROM THE MESOPOTAMIAN CONTEXT

Just as Moses needed to correct the theology of the Egyptian worldview for Israel, so he needed to correct the theology they had learned from Mesopotamia. Israel would have been familiar with the theology and worldview of Mesopotamia because of their ancestry in Abraham and, more so, because the worldview of Mesopotamia pervaded the ancient Near East. In fact, when the Israelites finally settled in Canaan, they would have confronted even more compelling expressions of the Mesopotamian worldview. Israel needed to know the God they served and his radical distinction from all the gods of the ancient Near East.

Like the Egyptian creation accounts, the Mesopotamian stories present a very different picture from the biblical accounts, especially with respect to the description of God. As we observed in the comparison and contrast of Genesis 1 with the Egyptian accounts, the God of the Bible is unique, transcendent above all of creation, and alone in the realm of deity. The different worldview of the Mesopotamian creation stories will further highlight that the God of Israel was not a created deity in quest of rule or trying to protect other gods from a raging dragon (Marduk's struggle with Tiamat). In contrast to all the ancient Near Eastern gods,

God was neither a part of the creation nor did he represent an abstract power.

Initial Conditions of Creation

Genesis 1:2   Desolate, empty, darkness, deep

Mesopotamia   Infinite(?) watery chaos, (darkness?)

Strictly speaking, the Mesopotamian accounts do not include all of the precreation qualities that the biblical and Egyptian accounts present, nor is the character of those qualities the same. Water dominates the scene in all three worldviews, but in Mesopotamia, the darkness is only implied and the extent of the precreation state is uncertain. With respect to these initial conditions of creation in Mesopotamian accounts, Genesis 1 makes the same points that it did with the Egyptian accounts. First, Israel's God is unique and transcendent, in distinction from the Mesopotamian gods that each represents an aspect of creation. He has absolute power, whereas Mesopotamian Marduk is powerful but not powerful enough to confront the raging deep without magical utterances and the weapons made by other gods. He only has relative power and needs the help of others to defeat a raging enemy. In Genesis 1, by contrast, God merely speaks and effortlessly brings light into darkness, vitalizes the desolation, and fills the emptiness.

This leads us to a second significant difference. Comparisons of Genesis 1 with the Mesopotamian accounts have led many scholars to assume that Genesis also reflects a struggle in creation. But the "deep" in Genesis 1:2 does not portray either a deity or an enemy in conflict with God. It is merely part of God's creation under God's sovereign spoken control.[1] Moses presents God as completely independent of creation and in absolute, effortless control. There is no struggle for control, no battle with various weapons and magic, no uncertain outcome to determine the king of the gods. Instead, Israel's God simply speaks into the dark, watery deep and brings forth light, order, and a good creation, demonstrating his preexisting rule. Genesis 1 gives no hint of a creation that results from cosmic conflict.

Levels of the universe are visible on this unfinished Babylonian boundary marker (housed in the Louvre), including the pillars of the earth and a serpent (a symbol of Marduk) in the deep below the earth. (Photo credit: Rama/Wikimedia Commons, courtesy of the Louvre)

Means of Creation

Genesis 1	God creates by divine command and "making"
Mesopotamia	Marduk destroys and restores a constellation with his word; creation is done by crafting

In Genesis 1, God's creation is accomplished by his word and by his "making" of things. While God separates the waters with a word in Genesis, in Mesopotamia, Marduk can neither subdue nor separate Tiamat with a word. He has to engage in an all-out battle to defeat her.

In fact none of the accounts from Mesopotamia presents anything of the actual creation of the universe as being accomplished by divine command.[2] When Marduk destroys and restores a constellation with his word, he is showing his destiny and divine supremacy over all the gods.[3] When it comes to the initial creating of the cosmos, however, "the creators are consistently represented after the manner of men (except that they are endowed with superhuman size and power) who bring things into existence by means of physical work, as the Lord God is portrayed in the second chapter of Genesis."[4]

As we saw in the Egyptian view of their gods, the ultimate demonstration of sovereignty—the role of the king and gods—was to bring about reality by their spoken word.[5] In Mesopotamia, divine supremacy for Marduk is linked to the divine command. In the biblical account, God indisputably demonstrates his sovereign control over all by the word of his command. The biblical account focuses on the creative word as the primary means of creation. The description of God "making" the elements of creation is secondary to his spoken creative acts.

Light Before Luminaries

Genesis 1:3–5, 14–18   God creates light on day 1 before the luminaries on day 4

Mesopotamia   Light, day, and night exist before the luminaries are created

The presence of light in *Enuma Elish* is inferred, not directly stated. Ancient Mesopotamia shows the consistent ancient perception of light independent from luminaries. In *Enuma Elish*, the light assumed in the day and night is not presented as created but as simply existing. It is not an issue in the text.[6] In the biblical account, light is clearly a significant work of God in dispelling or setting boundaries for darkness.

In Mesopotamia, Marduk radiates light as one of his attributes, but this aura is not necessarily in the same category as the light on day 1 of Genesis. The difference between these accounts appears clearly in the role and character of the light. In the biblical creation account, God creates light. Light is not portrayed as an attribute of God but as his creation, subject to his word.[7] God speaks light into existence and separates it from the darkness. It is under his control and distinct from his being.

Separation as the Initial Act of Creation

Genesis 1:6–8	God creates by separating the waters to create an atmosphere
Mesopotamia	The gods create by separating the waters to create an atmosphere

In the Mesopotamian accounts, as in the Egyptian creation, separating the waters is an initial motif in creation, but there are obvious significant differences between the ancient Near Eastern accounts and Genesis 1. We have already mentioned that the Genesis account is completely without conflict and without any sense of personification or deification of the "deep." God merely uses the waters in the Genesis account to begin the formation of a hospitable and inhabitable world. In Mesopotamia, by contrast, the separation of the waters is a terrible battle because it requires killing and dividing Tiamat.[8] Numerous scholars have looked for such a battle motif in the biblical accounts. However, not only does it not appear in Genesis 1, but such a theme is not clear in any of the Hebrew Bible.[9]

In addition, the creator gods in Mesopotamia are part of the creation, tied closely to it, and in continuing conflict with parts of it. According to the various cosmogonies, different gods are represented as creating—including Marduk, Anu, Ea, and Enlil, who represent the storm, sky, rivers, and air/weather, respectively. In addition to the direct creation, there is also secondary creation. So, for example, "Anu creates the heavens, the heavens create the earth, earth creates the rivers, the rivers create the canals, the canals create the marsh and the marsh creates the worm."[10] Genesis 1 clearly distinguishes its portrayal of God from these gods. He is outside of creation and in complete control.

With respect to the separation of the land from the waters, the Mesopotamian accounts do not present a clear and consistent picture. The land is not separated from the waters as it is in the biblical and Egyptian accounts, but it is built in some other way. In one account Marduk makes a raft on which he piles dirt to make the earth.[11] In another account, the heaven created the earth.[12] In most texts the creation of the earth is assumed and not described.

Creation of Sun, Moon, and Stars (and Light)

Genesis 1:14–18	God creates sun, moon, and stars for signs, seasons, days, and years, and to give light
Mesopotamia	The gods create sun, moon, and stars for signs, seasons, days, and years, and to give light

We noted earlier that the Genesis account does not name the luminaries and thereby does not name any of the gods of the ancient Near East, whether Mesopotamian, Egyptian, or Canaanite. While the general purposes for the luminaries are the same between the biblical and ancient Near Eastern perspectives, in the biblical account the lights are not deities. They are merely parts of God's creation, doing his bidding and accomplishing his will. They do not have independent rule or power in creation but are completely under God's control, doing his bidding.

On the other hand, Shamash, the Mesopotamian sun god, was associated with law and justice. The moon god, known as Sin or Nanna, was god of wisdom and was for a time king of the gods when Ur held control. Ur was one of the main places for moon worship (see the reconstructed ziggurat of Ur below, which was the main shrine to Nanna). By showing these "lights" to be merely aspects of his sovereign creation, God demonstrates his sovereign claim to justice and wisdom as well.

Creation of Mankind

Genesis 2:7	God formed man of the dust and breathed into him the breath of life
Mesopotamia	The gods formed man from clay (and the blood of a god) to do their work

Even though Genesis 2:7 is not in the creation account we are working with in this study (it is in the second section of Genesis that presents creation in significantly different ways than Genesis 1:1–2:3; see chapter 4 above), the portrayal of God forming man from the dust is worth noting. While the Mesopotamian cosmogony has many similarities with the biblical narrative in Genesis 2:4 through Genesis 11, a significant difference is evident in the creation of man. In Genesis 2 mankind serves God by working, but people are not relieving God of some intolerable load that he no longer can bear (as is the case in the Mesopotamian account). Instead, God creates man with the blessing and privilege of representing him, serving him, and entering into his rest.[13] In the Bible, people are not created to be slave labor, to satisfy the whims and needs of the gods; rather, they are kings and priests, serving in the temple of the transcendent Creator, enjoying his blessing and rest.

Another difference between Mesopotamia and Genesis 1 is worth noting. In Genesis 1, people are clearly presented as the image of God, a fact that is not true of the Mesopotamian accounts. As a result, the biblical purpose of man is vastly different from the Mesopotamian perception. The Mesopotamian gods create mankind specifically to do the work of the lesser gods and to relieve them from their misery and hard work. They can rest when man takes over. The biblical account, however, presents mankind as the vice-regent of God, representing God as his image in rule and authority over creation (Gen. 1:26–28).

God Rests

Genesis 2:1–3	God rests on the seventh day

| Mesopotamia | The gods rest after man is created, and gods typically rest in temples they build |

While the Genesis 1 account and the Mesopotamian accounts, like the Egyptian creation accounts, have a basic similarity in the fact of rest occurring after creation, the need for and meaning of rest in Mesopotamia are dramatically different. In the Mesopotamian accounts, the gods need rest because they are tired of working. They need relief from their labors. It comes after creation only because it is at that time that Marduk turns his attention to the needs of the gods and makes mankind in order to "bear the gods' burden that those may rest."[14] Rest for the gods has nothing to do with the creation itself outside of the need for slave labor in mankind. The God of the Bible (and similarly the gods in Egypt), however, rests in satisfaction because he has accomplished his work of creating and has established a good, ordered, and functioning world in which he holds sovereign control.[15] God, whose work in Genesis results from effortless commands, does not need relief, but, in fact, gains his own "relief" in day 7 apart from mankind's help.[16]

The biblical purpose of man is not to serve God by offering him relief but by offering appropriate worship and service, representing him in rule and authority on earth. In contrast to worship in the ancient Near East—namely, a way to meet the physical needs of the gods—worship in the Bible appropriately honors the sovereign king through service and recognition of his holy goodness. Israel's God, in contrast to the Mesopotamian gods, is interested in the well-being of mankind and so fashions a hospitable place for people. Marduk, as Ea before him, is interested only in the well-being of the gods and prepares places for temples so that the gods, including Marduk himself, can rest or be relieved of their burdens.[17]

God's rest presents a second contrastive issue. While the resting of the Mesopotamian gods in their temples as they administrate a peaceful kingdom closely matches the intent of Genesis 1, where God rests in his cosmic temple at the end of creation, there is an important difference in the scope of the creators' handiwork. All of creation is not seen as the

Saddam Hussein reconstructed a Ziggurat of Ur showing part of a temple complex meant to serve the needs of the gods. (Photo credit: Michael Lubinski/Wikimedia Commons)

temple of any Mesopotamian god. Marduk builds his temple after creation and within creation (as does Ea, who rests in it). For the God of the Bible, however, the heavens are his throne, the earth his footstool, and the entire created cosmos his temple of rest (Isa. 66:1). The significance of this distinction is critical to understanding the biblical perception of Yahweh. He alone deserves a temple, because he alone is deity. He alone rules creation and he rules the entire cosmos. All of the creation, then, is under his control as his sacred space.

Sequence of Events

Genesis 1:3–19   Out of desolate, empty, dark waters, God creates atmosphere, land, and luminaries in the heavens, followed by animals and man; then God rests

Mesopotamia	From primeval dark chaos the gods create atmosphere, land, and luminaries in the heavens (followed by animals and man); then the gods rest

As we saw with the Egyptian accounts, the differences in the sequence of creative events in Mesopotamia and Genesis 1 are not as much in the *order* of creation as such, but in the *impact* and *theological statement* being made. The biblical presentation of the nature of God, as already noted numerous times, reveals a unique God who stands in complete contrast to all the limited, finite, and humanlike gods of the ancient Near East. The biblical account allows no conflict or change in God, who is a totally sovereign and independent being, crafting all of creation to do his bidding.

A second significant difference in the presentation of creation relates to its timing. Although the sequence seems to be similar between Genesis 1 and creation in Mesopotamia, the Mesopotamian accounts consistently present creation as happening all at once and not over a period of seven days (or any other number of days). This is much like what we saw in the Egyptian accounts.[18] While seven is a common number for many events in the ancient Near East[19]—such as approaching the gods, carrying out missions, or waiting for designated periods—only Israel uses a seven-day week and has a Sabbath on every seventh day. We will return to this issue in chapter 12.

Purpose of the Creation Accounts

Genesis 1–2	God as creator claims sovereignty over all creation and so over all nations
Mesopotamia	Particular gods are presented as having authority over their realm of creation

Once again, we have to recognize the biblical difference in its contention for God's unique and sole supremacy. Moses does not recognize a competing pantheon of gods but presents all of creation, including the so-called gods of the other nations, as merely the product of God's creative word. Israel's God presents his sole and distinct claims for sovereign control of all of creation, including the submission and worship of all peoples.

We have already seen that Marduk's role in creation argues for his supremacy over all gods. On the other hand, some of the minor cosmogonies depict two creators, each creating his own half of the world (Anu [sky] and Ea [rivers and streams]), or three creators creating their own spheres (Anu, Ea, and Enlil [air and weather]).[20] The creators then claim control over what they created, including the lesser gods.

Summary

The distinctions between the biblical account of creation and those of Mesopotamia show the significant theological contrasts being drawn between the two worldviews. They also indicate the polemic in the Hebrew account against the prevailing worldview of Israel's neighbors. Israel needed to hear how their God was different from any god that the other peoples around them worshiped. They needed to have their worldview remade in light of a radically different encounter with the divine who was transcendent and sovereign over all aspects of creation.

The distinctions that Israel learns in Genesis 1 show the character of Yahweh to be transcendent—he is not part of creation but is unique and all-powerful. He is sovereign over all by the effortless word of his command; there is no struggle in creation. All creation—the product of God's sovereign, creative imagination, and under his effortless control—therefore answers to him. After creation, God rests in satisfaction in his well-ordered, functioning creation, rather than collapsing in exhaustion after his hard work. Within God's creation, mankind is not a slave but a kingly representative of the great King, whom people willingly worship in response to his greatness (not as a way to meet God's needs and make him comfortable, hoping to get something in return).

We see the same kinds of contrasts here as we saw in our discussion of the Egyptian materials, and all of the distinctions apply from the summary of chapter 8, except the specific contrast with the sun god of Egypt. Of particular distinction in the Mesopotamian cosmogony is the struggle that defines creation, a struggle completely absent in Genesis. God is effortlessly in control over a fully subservient creation. In addition, the purpose of Mesopotamian man is radically different from biblical people. Mankind is not created to meet God's needs but to represent him and lead creation in worship of the God who meets all mankind's needs. We might then summarize the obvious distinctions this way:

1. God in Genesis exists independently of creation and is not created or self-created.
2. God transcends creation.
3. God is effortlessly sovereign over all creation without struggle.
4. God alone is deity.
5. Israel was to celebrate the rule of God in their lives by imitating their creator in work and rest each week.
6. Man does not provide for God, but God provides for man.

The Mesopotamian creation materials remind us that Genesis 1 uses basic ancient conceptions of the material world to describe creation, but it recasts their theology to refute directly the mythological mindset of the people with whom Israel interacted. Israel needed to learn the sovereign, transcendent nature of their God—a God unlike any god in Mesopotamia or anywhere else in the ancient Near East.[21] By learning about this God, the Israelites also learned the reason for their necessary submission and service to him as their King. The creation account of Genesis 1 powerfully refutes common theological concepts of the ancient Near East—Egypt, Israel's home for more than four hundred years; Mesopotamia, a broadly influential culture; and even the neighbors nearest to Israel's new home. It is to the Canaanites we now turn.

Chapter Eleven

GENESIS 1 AND THE CANAANITE CONTEXT

One other source of dangerous theology that may have threatened the Israelites was Canaan, the land to which Israel was moving after their exodus from Egypt. In Genesis 1, Moses might have been disputing theology that stemmed from the Canaanites' view of creation, in addition to the theologies of Egypt and Mesopotamia. Canaan had been home to Abraham, Isaac, Jacob, and their families before Israel's long sojourn in Egypt. Was there ongoing memory of the gods of Canaan during Israel's long absence in Egypt? Is there any evidence that the desire to counter Canaanite beliefs influenced the writing of Genesis 1? The Canaanite evidence is actually weak with regard to creation accounts, since we know little about Canaanite cosmogony. However, we do know that Canaanite gods were well represented in Egypt and that Canaanite beliefs would become significant to Israel in the centuries to come.

The Creator(s)

Very little can be said with certainty about Canaanite creation parallels, since there are no clear cosmogonies in the Canaanite materials to date. Little is known about creation beyond the title of *creator* given

On the back of a knife handle from Gebel el-Arak (housed in the Louvre), El is pictured between two lions. El was head of the Canaanite pantheon and was called "creator" of heaven and earth. (Photo credit: Rama/Wikimedia Commons, courtesy of the Louvre)

to the god El and the goddess Asherah, his wife. El was the head of the Canaanite pantheon, along with his consort, Asherah. He is described as creator of the earth, of gods, and of men, while Asherah shares in creating the gods. Beyond those titles, nothing is clearly known as to the means of creation, its timing, or relationships among the gods and what they created (see figure 11).[1]

El is a generic name for "god" in the Canaanite region, and could be used in different circumstances with different connotations. For instance, Melchizedek was a priest of El-Elyon, the Most High God (Gen. 14:18). Hagar called the name of "Yahweh who spoke to her," El-Roeh, the God who sees me (Gen. 16:13). The use of *El* in that era may be similar to the use of *Allah* today. *Allah* is a common name for God in Arabic. When a person with a Muslim background becomes a

This crude clay Asherah, the wife of El and cocreator of the gods, indicates how common her worship was. (Photo credit: John Soden, courtesy of Lancaster Bible College)

follower of Jesus Christ, he may still use the name *Allah* for God, but he has to fill it with different meaning. There may be religious, cultural, and emotional attachments that come with the name, and continued use of it may create confusion over who God really is. This was certainly the case with the identity and character of Yahweh in ancient Israel, as seen both through the biblical descriptions and the picture of life during the period of Israel's monarchy presented by archaeology. Whether or not Israel equated Yahweh with Baal and/or El of the Canaanite pantheon, they definitely combined his worship with worship of other deities.[2]

Despite his elevated position as creator, El did not dominate the Canaanite pantheon. In fact, he was eclipsed by his son, Baal. Baal was a storm god who became a fertility god. For the pagan Canaanites, Baal

Baal, god of the storm, aided the fertility of the ground through the rains. (Photo credit: Jastrow/ Wikimedia Commons, courtesy of the Louvre)

held the key to continued life and the economy because their agricultural lifestyle depended upon the recurrent rains.

Baal was not the creator but was birthed by the creator, El. The Baal myth relates battles between Baal and the Sea (Yamm) and Death (Mot). Scholars have looked for connections between these and creation stories, but no evidence is yet available to show any clear relationship.[3] Similar motifs in biblical passages are sometimes used to argue that the Bible sees creation as a cosmic struggle between Yahweh and the elements (sea, death, aridity). A careful look at the biblical accounts, however, does not support this sort of struggle in God's creation of the universe.[4]

Figure 11. Gods of Canaan	
Asherah	• the wife of El • cocreator of the gods
Astarte	• the goddess of fertility, sexuality, and war • associated with the evening star
Baal	• the god of storm and thus also the god of fertility
El	• general Semitic word for "god" • creator and ruler of the gods • creator of earth and heaven, including mankind • husband of Asherah
Mot	• the god of death
Qedeshet	• a fertility goddess • also called Qetesh
Resheph	• a god of plague and war
Yamm	• the god of the sea

But while Baal was not the creator, he was believed to control an aspect of creation, the weather. Canaanites served him in search of rain, and Israelites were deeply influenced by Baal worshipers. This is why drought and storm are so significant, for example, in the conflict between Elijah and the prophets of Baal (1 Kings 17–18). Both the prophet's words and God's works proved that Baal had no control over the true Creator, the God of Israel, nor over any of his creation. It was Yahweh alone who had brought everything into being and caused it to function according to his will. Yahweh had put the atmosphere and weather into place (day 2 of creation). The clouds are his chariot, the winds his messengers (Ps. 104:3–4, a creation psalm) rather than Baal's. Lightning bolts are his arrows (Ps. 18:13–14). The one who created nature also controls nature. Futato has argued that the description of Yahweh as the giver of rain (Gen. 2:5) was intended to predispose Israel against Baal.[5] The Canaanite gods would have been well understood by Moses, since they are well represented and pictured in the archaeological discoveries from his time period in Egypt.[6] It is certainly possible that Moses intended to counter Canaanite theology in Genesis.

While Baal is not the creator in the Baal myth, and the myth does not

present an ordered account of creation, there still may be clues to the cosmogony of the Canaanites. The three daughters of Baal in the myth represent Baal's control over the three aspects of fertility: light, rain, and earth.
In Averbeck's analysis, the elements dealt with on the first three days of
Genesis 1 correspond "exactly to the names of Baal's three daughters,
which correspond to the three fundamental structures or elements of the
cosmos: light, sky/rain, and earth/dry ground."[7] These three are basic, initial elements in Canaanite creation, similar to the beginning of creation
in days 1 through 3 in Genesis 1 (light, atmosphere, and land being separated). In addition, in the Baal myth, light is not the same as the luminaries
and exists independently, as in Genesis 1.[8] The similarities are significant
because they indicate that there may have been a common perception
across the ancient world of some of these initial qualities of creation.

Summary

While the Canaanite literature offers very little help in understanding
the people's perspective on creation itself, it does make very clear that
the Canaanites had a polytheistic worldview—a fundamental difference between Canaanite and Israelite theology. Thus the same theological distinctions that the biblical creation account provides against the
Egyptian or Mesopotamian perceptions of their multiple gods would be
equally effective against the Canaan worldview.

The biblical accounts resoundingly dismiss the concept of deified
elements of creation by treating all of creation as devoid of personality
and totally subservient to the spoken will of God. The theology of the
Canaanites relied on viewing the gods as equal to various elements of the
cosmos, possessing power to be exploited (or avoided) by the savvy worshiper. Moses' description of the elements, such as the "greater and lesser
lights," without naming the sun or moon, would speak as loudly against
the Canaanite deities as it did against the Egyptian or Mesopotamian
deities. In addition, the way Genesis 2 highlights God's role in supplying
rain to produce crops (v. 5) would have been particularly significant in
Canaan with its theology of Baal as the storm god and resulting fertility.[9]

Part 3

THE SIGNIFICANCE OF THE CREATION ACCOUNT FOR THEOLOGY TODAY

Chapter Twelve

OBJECTIONS (PART 1)

Truth and Chronology

"Daddy, where do babies come from?" your five-year-old asks from the back seat of the car. You weigh your answer. You could tell her about the egg and sperm, the process of conception, the genetics involved with RNA and DNA, chromosomes and what makes boys or girls, the process of the fertilized egg implanting, growing, developing, and all the finer points of gestation, up to the point of birth. Of course, that would be way too much information. Maybe all she needs to know is "From the hospital, not from a stork!" What you really want her to understand at her age is that God makes a baby in Mommy's tummy, and when it is time, Mommy will go to the hospital and bring home the baby. If you tried to explain the science of reproduction to your little daughter, she would have no idea what you were talking about. Not only would it be too much information, it would also confuse her, and she would undoubtedly miss the one thing you really want her to understand—that every birth represents a miracle.

In a similar sort of way, God chose not to correct all of the incorrect perceptions of the world held by his people throughout their history. In a prescientific age, Israel would have not only missed the point of such instruction but would have been unable to understand and process a modern scientific explanation. For that matter, which "scientific" explanation would God have given them? As we mentioned earlier, our science has changed dramatically over the past century (not to mention the last 3,000 years) and will continue to change as scientific observations and data escalate exponentially and the scientific community presents better and better—or even totally different—ways of explaining the data available. Even today, if we talked about quantum physics or string theory to most people in an average church, their eyes would quickly glaze over. They might be confused or bored, and they would certainly not be engaged. They would not only miss the point we were making, they would probably not even care what that point was.

As we process what we have just observed about Genesis 1 and the ancient Near Eastern creation accounts, we see that God does correct wrong theology, but his instruction does not depend upon accurate scientific observations and descriptions of the material world. This reality fits well with the concept of progressive revelation—the idea that God slowly revealed himself within the cultural framework his people knew. We can see this at work in the social order when we observe that God did not immediately correct Israel's perceptions of multiple wives or slavery.[1] The same principle is at work in his revelation of creation. God used their "language"—in this case their language about creation—to reveal truth they could not otherwise know.

We have already suggested that a number of exegetical details allow for and even point to a broadly figurative approach to Genesis 1 rather than a "literal" chronological approach. The chronologies of chapters 1 and 2 are not the same and so at least one of them (and possibly both) must be understood as nonlinear in its presentation. Traditionally we have understood chapter 2 to be out of chronological order because it is second and does not have the markers of "one day . . . a second day," and so on. However, there are parallels between the chapters and other clues that have led some Hebrew scholars to conclude that neither chapter is ordered chronologically.[2] Clearly both chapters are carefully arranged and crafted to present theological points, which does not automatically mean they are not chronological, but it may suggest we ought to pay attention to the theological points without assuming a strict linear chronology. In Genesis 1 we noted the odd absence of the article in the first five days, and then how the article with day 6 clearly emphasizes that day; this suggests the possibility that the narrative does not give a linear chronology but is, in fact, arguing particularly against an Egyptian worldview. Day 7 is missing the final formula, "there was evening and there was morning, the seventh day." This indicates, at the very least, a significant difference in the way day 7 is being portrayed and may additionally indicate the ongoing rest of God, as Hebrews 4:1–11 seems to indicate. This line of thinking would argue for a figurative understanding of the whole week.

Many of the details in Genesis 1 clearly correlate with ancient Near Eastern perceptions, especially the Egyptian viewpoint: the initial conditions from which God creates, his means of creating by his word, the presence of light before the luminaries (days 1 and 4), the separation of the light from the darkness, the separation of the waters above the expanse from the waters below, the order of the events, the making of man in the image of God, and God resting. We suggested that the biblical account is forcefully refuting the perception of deities among Israel's pagan neighbors, from Egypt to Mesopotamia and including Canaan. As Gerhard Hasel states, Genesis 1 presents "not only a 'complete break' with the ancient Near Eastern mythological cosmologies," but also fully rejects their theology with "a conscious and deliberate antimythical polemic," intended to destroy their worldview.[3]

But what do the parallels tell us about the chronology of creating, and, more specifically, how the account aligns with any particular scientific perspective? If indeed Moses did not attempt to refute the Israelites' prescientific mind-set, but instead used their perceptions of creation to establish a strong theology of God's transcendent nature, it dramatically impacts our own attempts to correlate Genesis 1 with the science of today—or the science of any time period. For example, if Genesis 1 intends to begin with the common ancient Near Eastern viewpoint—particularly the Egyptian view—of the precreation watery dark chaos, then the narrative does not accord with any modern science. If Genesis leaves intact the ancient conclusion of endless waters above the sky and below the earth, without correcting that inference from observation with the reality of a space that is billions of light-years of emptiness, then it is not concerned to present a correct version of what science might

How could Israel in Egypt have understood an accurate account of the universe, and how would they have then understood an accurate theology in distinction from their neighbors' beliefs? (Photo credit: Rebekah Fry/ NASA/Reto Stöckli/Robert Simmon/MODIS)

later validate. It simply does not speak to the scientific questions of today or any day. Instead, Genesis presents theological truth: Yahweh is Creator, transcendent and absolute sovereign over all. He is not part of creation but completely separate from it.

If God had tried to correct Israel's observation and perception of the material world, would it have made sense to the people in their historical context? They had no background for such an understanding. Would they have identified with a modern scientific understanding of the cosmos any more than a five-year-old can identify with and understand a medical description of the initiation, growth, and birth of a baby brother or sister? Would they not have missed the relevance of God's crucial message about his nature and about their purpose and response to him— and still not have understood the scientific reality of their universe? They would not have seen the application of Genesis 1 to their cultural and historical framework—the way it challenged the pagan perceptions of their neighbors and gave them the truth to withstand the idolatry of their contemporaries. Instead, God chose to connect with them on a level that they could understand. He put his theology in terms they would expect and to which they could relate, so that they could effectively compare the theology with the religious competition. In other words, God corrected their spiritual worldview, not their physical picture of the world, by teaching them who Yahweh their God was (Exod. 6:6–7). He began with the way they thought and talked about creation, in order to teach them what they could not otherwise recognize or understand.

Averbeck suggests a similar conclusion in his evaluation of the connection between Genesis 1 and the cosmogony underlying the Baal epic. He recognizes the same natural order in the Canaanite cosmogony as in the first three days of Genesis 1 with light, atmosphere, and earth appearing before the sun, moon, and stars, and he concludes that "as strange as it may sound to us, for them there had to be light before there were lights. This is just how they thought and talked about it, so the Genesis 1 account simply starts there but adds to the three days with another three that went further, thus making it six days."[4]

If the details of the creation as revealed in Genesis 1 accord with the Israelites' prescientific worldview rather than with our modern scientific worldview, and if the events reflect what the people may have learned in Egypt, then why should we try to turn them into modern science? Or why should we try to make modern science accord with them? Genesis 1 does not have to fit science and science does not have to fit Genesis 1. We believe that God's intent was not to affirm a particular description of the process of creation but instead to affirm his particular character as the Creator. God is the absolute creator of everything. He does not provide a scientific explanation of how he created—that was not the point.

Our conclusion raises some important questions that need responses.

How can I trust the Bible if it does not mean what it says?

Now we are back to the beginning. The question, however, is not, "How can I trust the Bible if it does not mean what it says?" What this question is really asking is, "Can I trust the Bible if it does not mean what I thought it meant from my context when I initially read it, before I understood what it would have meant to the original readers?" We have already established the principle that the authority and reliability of God's Word is based on what it affirms. Affirmation must be understood in light of what God said through the original author to the original audience—how they would have understood its meaning. We cannot force the text to say what we want it to say without doing violence to God's intent and the medium of normal human communication. Our job is to discover the meaning that God intended for the original audience, so that we can apply it truthfully and fruitfully to subsequent audiences in all ages (2 Tim. 3:14–17). Then we will know that we are hearing the Word of God, and we can trust his intended message. This message will not be different from what the original audience would have understood.

There are those in the church today who believe that the meaning of the text rises above the culture and humanity of the human author and original recipients so that only the text is necessary to understand the meaning.[5] But as Younger points out, such a position clearly misunderstands the traditional view on the perspicuity (clarity) of Scripture.[6] Believing that the common person can clearly understand and interpret Scripture does not mean that all other resources should not or do not have to be brought to bear in the interpretation (such as the original languages, for example); rather, it means that with the proper resources, anyone can accurately determine the meaning and intent of Scripture. The interpreter does not have to be sanctioned by the church and does not have to discover some hidden teaching. However, it is necessary to understand all aspects of the original context, because human communication, which God has chosen to use, is deeply rooted in historical, cultural, and linguistic contexts.

The burden is on us to understand the message in its original context and not in ours. If we fail to recognize and properly use the cultural and historical context of the Bible, we are likely to discover incorrect meaning and develop inappropriate theology. Consider a creative pastor who tries to develop theology from fiction such as *The Hobbit* or *Lord of the Rings*. The pastor might discover some theological truth and interesting correlations in the books, but ultimately, his efforts will break down. The books may illustrate theology, but they are not theology. This is not the author's fault; he didn't intend to write theology. In a similar way, God didn't intend his instruction to Israel to be science. There may be some correlations between the Bible and science, but when the science breaks down, it is not God's fault. He was not writing a scientific manual.

If you claim that Genesis 1 uses erroneous ancient views to challenge Israel's belief in God, don't you undermine the doctrine of inspiration and inerrancy?

This question about inspiration and inerrancy incorrectly assumes that using the inaccurate views of people (either in passing or in polemic) is the same as affirming those views. If we believed that the intent of the author was to affirm that view, then we would have a problem with inerrancy. Millard Erickson defines inerrancy: "The Bible, when correctly interpreted in light of the level to which culture and the means of communication had developed at the time it was written, and in view of the purposes for which it was given, is fully truthful in all that it affirms."[7] He then lists several principles and illustrations to "help us to define inerrancy more specifically and to remove some of the difficulties."[8]

We have already illustrated that using an observation of how the world functions, even if the reader or hearer believes it to be true (such as talking about the sun rising), does not constitute error. The writer uses his audience's understanding (or way of talking about it) in order to make an argument or to teach a significant point.[9] The observations of the Egyptians had led to a certain understanding of the universe, which Genesis does not challenge. How would the Israelites have understood the science or the theology of Genesis 1 if God had spoken in terms of a relative (Einsteinian) view of the universe? And what if the Einsteinian view of the universe is not accepted a hundred years from now? Will this affect the meaning of Genesis 1? God is not affirming the Egyptian view of the universe and creation, but rather he is using it for polemical purposes and as a teaching tool to affirm his place as creator. He does not intend to affirm the events or order of creation. He is affirming his claim to be the Creator.

Perhaps this situation is somewhat similar to Jesus' statement that the smallest seed is the mustard seed (Mark 4:31). The mustard seed is not, however, the absolutely smallest seed known to us. But in his cultural context, Jesus did not correct the common conviction of the people; instead he used it to teach a point about the kingdom of God—it starts small and will grow large! We don't accuse him of error because the mustard seed is not the smallest seed known to man, but we acknowledge the cultural context and perspective of his hearers, as well as the proverbial status of the mustard seed.

In addition to the ancient Near Eastern cosmology present in Genesis 1, a second issue is the seven-day week. We will discuss this further below, but at this point let us say that this issue also comes down to the intended meaning of the author. People in the ancient world often did not expect history writing to have precise chronology.

Additionally, the use of a seven-day pattern occurs consistently in symbolic ways throughout the ancient Near East. By drawing from Israel's context, God claims that all of creation is under his absolute control and is moving toward his ultimate goal. His claim is similar to—but far beyond—the claims made throughout Egypt's history by each succeeding claimant to the status of creator. While several Egyptian gods are put in the role of creator throughout Egyptian history, none claims exclusive and absolute authority over all aspects of creation. Israel's God makes a very powerful statement to his Egyptianized people about his exclusive role in the theological universe.

The issue in Genesis 1 is not inerrancy but understanding the intent of the author and what he affirms. If the original author intended the account to be understood figuratively or symbolically, then we would be in error to ascribe a literal meaning to it. If the original author used his audience's incorrect descriptions in order to make theological points, we would be wrong to expect his writing to correct their vocabulary or perceptions. Inspiration and inerrancy are concerned with intent and affirmation.

But wouldn't it be misleading for God to say creation occurred in seven days if it really didn't?

Why would God frame creation in seven days if they were not literal? Wouldn't he be misleading us? The problem here is also one of intent. Did God intend to give Israel a chronology of creation? We have observed a number of clues in the text that suggest perhaps God was not giving Israel a chronology of the events in creation but rather was framing creation theologically. What might have been his intent in doing this?

There is no known record of any other society framing creation in seven days, so the use of it in Genesis 1 does not appear to be directly dependent on Israel's ancient Near Eastern mind-set.[10] The use of a seven-day period of time, however, commonly appears in ancient Near Eastern mythology, legend, and cultic practice.[11] For example, it occurs to describe an appropriate approach to the gods;[12] it provides a framework for a divinely ordained and successful mission to find a royal wife to bear a son;[13] and it describes a seven-day waiting period, in which the anticipated event occurs on the seventh day.[14] The number seven was also frequently used for many other things in the ancient texts (and even in the Hebrew Old Testament) and was not always intended to be a literal number; instead, it carried symbolic significance, being generally understood to express the ideas of completion, perfection, or fulfillment.[15]

In addition to its use of "seven" or "seven days" as a rhetorical device, the ancient Near Eastern world did not sharply distinguish between their stories of cosmogony and "history." Neither cosmogony (how the universe came to be) nor cosmology (how one understands the universe, including the relationship of the gods) in the ancient world was understood in scientific or historical terms but as symbolic, metaphysical explanations or as a means to "articulate the incomprehensible and the marvelous, while attempting to express such phenomena in a rational manner."[16]

We are not saying that Genesis 1 is untrue. We are suggesting that by borrowing the events of Egyptian cosmogony and placing them in a seven-day framework, the author was emphasizing the theological significance for the nation of Israel. He was not making a statement about what he considered to be (or what God considered to be) a historical timeline, particularly one based on the precision our modern minds require. With its context in ancient Egypt, Israel would not have required or expected a strict (modern) historical correlation. The seven days of creation clearly devastate the theology of the Egyptian "first time" or single day of creation that is reenacted every day. The Genesis 1 framework of seven days deliberately countered any theological misperceptions of sacred time and developed the purpose and plan of their creator.

If God is giving the creation account to Israel shortly after they leave Egypt, he is also giving them the Ten Commandments at approximately the same time. When he defines their responsibilities as his people, he includes keeping the Sabbath as one of the foundational commands of his new kingdom and the sign of their covenant together (Exod. 20:8–11; 31:12–17). They were to keep Sabbath as the external evidence of their participation in their covenant relationship with Yahweh.[17] The people were to keep Sabbath in imitation of their king. Just as God created heaven and earth in six days and rested on the seventh, so Israel should demonstrate its participation in his kingdom, under his sovereign rule, by working six days and resting on the seventh day.

When the instruction is repeated in Exodus 31:12–17, we get a clue that God's rest on the seventh day was figurative and not literal. God was "refreshed" by his rest (v. 17), although none of us would say he was exhausted after his week of work. Rather, God described his work-week in a way that corresponded with human experience. He intended it to be an anthropomorphic description. Throughout Genesis 1 God deliberately states creation in terms of Israel's experience, not only to undermine the theology of Egypt (see chapters 7–8) but also to provide a means for Israel to enjoy his sovereignty and their submission in his kingdom on a weekly basis. Israel's very existence should have reminded them of their need for God because of the six-day struggle for existence each week (Gen. 3:17–19) and the need for relief or "rest" from the curse (Gen. 5:28–29). The celebration of Sabbath, unique to Israel in the ancient Near East, was God's provision for such rest. It provided another tangible way for them to be distinct, holy to their God. Just as the King rested in satisfaction at creating a good universe that functioned effectively, so his faithful subjects were to demonstrate their submission to his sovereign rule and their participation in his rest.[18]

The use of the seven-day week to describe creation would have had one additional effect for the Israelites. It liberated the concept of time from dependency upon natural phenomena, specifically the waxing and waning of the moon, the rising of the sun, and the harvest season. Pagan societies typically based time on these natural events, which were all associated with gods. By giving Israel a seven-day week that culminated with rest and the worship of Yahweh, God provided Israel with a means of calculating time independently of the pagan deities. Instead time itself was focused on the Creator.

If God changed the order of events from the Egyptian description, shouldn't that lead us to believe he was correcting a wrong order?

This expectation that God was correcting an incorrect order of events grows out of our modern expectations rather than out of the nature of the ancient Near Eastern mind-set or texts. We suggested in chapter 8 that Genesis 1 functions as an introduction to the rest of the story, particularly the more focused account of the creation (Gen. 2) with the resulting fall narrative (Gen. 3). Such a literary theological purpose for the framing of the account would not require a strict chronology. In fact, Genesis 1–11 deviates several times from a strict chronological sequence: Genesis 2 goes back and retells creation from a different perspective, at least beginning with day 6; Genesis 4 goes well beyond Genesis 5 with its genealogy of Cain and its account of Lamech; the genealogy of Genesis 10 goes well beyond the story of Babel in chapter 11 and describes the basic relation of Israel to its neighbors.

Those of us who live in Western societies generally assume that narrative will be chronological. This is not always the case in the Hebrew Scriptures, however, as illustrated above in Genesis 1–11. The book of Judges provides another example of narrative that is not strictly chronological. At the very least, many of the judges overlap since the total number of years of judging, oppression, and rest total many more than anyone's chronology of the period of time for the book. The order of arrangement may be topical rather than chronological in order to show the downward spiral of Israel. Furthermore, the order of the tribes from which the judges originate—beginning with Judah and concluding with Dan—relate to the general order of the conquest narratives in Joshua and Judges 1. Finally, the concluding narratives (chapters 17–21) may be out of order, providing a theological summary of the conditions that dominated the entire period.[19] Second Samuel provides another example of chronological discontinuity. The events of chapter 8 (David's wars) seem to be recorded thematically in order to show the fulfillment of God's promise of victory for David, even though the wars occurred at various times in David's reign. The same is true in the New Testament. For instance, the order of the temptations of Christ is different in Matthew 4 and Luke 4. The temptations are the same, but Matthew places the test on the pinnacle of the temple second, while Luke puts it third. Each had his purpose, and no one at the time they wrote would have accused either of being historically inaccurate.

The point is that narratives are not always chronological in the Bible, contrary to our expectations.[20] Even more to the point are the previous comments on the ancient people's expectation with regard to a historical/scientific correspondence in their cosmological texts. If the ancient audience did not expect or require a historical/scientific correspondence in Genesis 1, then changing the order of events or crafting it in seven days would not necessarily be aimed at giving a scientific (or historical) correction to a close but slightly off Egyptian view. Instead, as we have argued, it would more likely provide a theological correction.

Should we not assume that Genesis 1 is so similar to the other accounts, particularly the Egyptian material, because all the accounts came from Noah by oral tradition, and Genesis tells the true account, while the others mix it with idolatry and corrupt it?

The possibility of a common source for all of the similarities in the ancient Near Eastern traditions is a long-standing proposal. Heidel considered the possibilities of just such a tie between Genesis and *Enuma Elish*, citing Ira Price from the University of Chicago before him.[21] It is certainly reasonable to suggest that Israel may have had an oral tradition, passed down for centuries, that was used by Moses—an oral tradition that would have been similar to the Egyptian account (or Mesopotamian). However, if we are hoping thereby to discover a "scientific" sort of account, or something that can be used to correct "science," we will still be disappointed. Moses does not attempt to correct the assumptions Israel would have had regarding the waters above the (solid) expanse, or to describe the earth as a globe, or the relation of land to water, or the state of the universe, or the place of the earth in space, and so on. Instead he uses descriptions that incorporate their prescientific mind-set. We have to wonder, then, why he would correct the number of days of creation when he does not correct the other misconceptions. Instead he leaves intact a completely different view of the universe that is scientifically incorrect.

Leaving their perceptions in place and using their vocabulary to talk about it is not significantly different from what we often do with "observational speech." When we say the "sun rose" today, we use an expression that may very well go back to a time when it was believed that the sun actually rose. That does not mean, however, that we are trying to deceive or that we are ignorant about the universe, but only that we are using a common expression to communicate the beginning of daylight. We recognize the discrepancy, yet we do not feel the need to correct the science of everyone who uses the expression. Jesus himself, as we noted earlier, did not try to correct the same misconception even though no one in his audience could have known the real truth of the movements of the sun relative to the earth (Matt. 5:45). Perhaps this is similar to what God is doing in Genesis 1. The normal perception of the ancient world was based on their observations. While they did not know better (i.e., have a scientific explanation), God still did not see the need to challenge their observations. Their way of speaking about the physical universe was the best platform for describing a corrected theology.

While it may be possible that the ancient Near Eastern creation accounts came from a common source, there are clues that seem to make it less likely. If all the stories had come from a single source that looked much like what we read in Genesis, it is very strange that not a single one outside of Genesis includes the seven days of creation, given the prevalence of the use of "seven" in the ancient world. Not a single account elsewhere includes the seventh-day Sabbath concept. In fact, the basic flow of time in the ancient Near East is usually based on the lunar calendar, not the week as it is in Genesis. Since Genesis was the last account written down, it seems unlikely that all other peoples would have dropped the week and the Sabbath if it was originally understood to be so significant. In fact, if it came through Noah, and then probably through Abraham, wouldn't we expect to see some evidence that he and his family had observed Sabbath long before the Law? Finally, Exodus 31 states that the Sabbath is given specifically to Israel as a sign of their covenant, not a general requirement for all peoples. It comes at the giving of the creation story to Israel, suggesting that this may be the purpose for relating the seven days to mankind.

Conclusion

It is a natural, understandable tendency to import our cultural expectations into our reading, rather than to see through the eyes of the original audience. But to be accurate biblically, we need to put ourselves into the original audience's sandals, try to hear with their ears, and try to listen with their expectations and perceptions. We have strong clues that the Genesis account is not a scientific account when we consider how God has contextualized his instruction to Israel's perceptions of the material world. Genesis 1 flows out of a picture of the world that is, in fact, contrary to what most of us recognize with our modern understanding. Thus we are not free to use Genesis 1 to evaluate our science or to promote a special view of science. While there may be some correlations with modern science, the point of the passage is to be found in its theology. This is not to deny that Yahweh is creator but to recognize that he has not revealed to us in Genesis 1 the details or mechanics of that creation.

Chapter Thirteen

OBJECTIONS (PART 2)

The Meanings of Day *and* Death

I f you grew up in a traditional, conservative church, you have heard the story of creation repeated fairly concisely. The earth was created in six literal days. The first man, Adam, was created on the sixth day, and then his wife, Eve, was created. Shortly after that, he and his wife sinned against God under the influence of Satan. Their judgment was death, and they were expelled from the garden of Eden. Creation also was affected adversely by their judgment with the beginning of animal and plant death. All humans and all of creation have suffered the results of this judgment ever since.

This story has been repeated so often that to suggest that the earth may be old, which would entail plant and animal death *before* Adam and Eve sinned, seems diametrically opposed to the Bible itself. But is it? In this chapter we'll offer alternative explanations for those parts of the creation account that seem to argue most strongly for a recent, literal six days. The purpose is not to support a relatively old earth scientifically but to show that we are free to explore the scientific evidence wherever it may lead, without the accusation that we are being unfaithful to biblical teaching.

The Use of the Word *Day*

All Bible scholars agree that the Hebrew word *day* (*yom*) can mean something other than a twenty-four-hour period. For instance, it is used in Genesis 1:5 and 1:14 to refer only to the daylight hours. In Genesis 2:4 it refers to the whole "week" or period of creation: "This is the account of the heavens and the earth when they were created, *in the day* that the LORD God made earth and heaven" (NASB, emphasis added).[1] In Job 14:6 *yom* is used figuratively to refer to a man's entire lifetime. And *yom* is used over and over in the prophetic books to refer to an indefinite period of judgment, "the day of the LORD" (e.g., Isa. 2:12; Zeph. 1:7; Zech. 14:1).

However, some Young Earth Creationists argue that the grammar of Genesis 1 necessitates that the word *day* be taken literally in that context. This is one of the reasons that they are convinced they must believe in a recent creation; in their minds, the Bible demands it. There are two main arguments behind this interpretation of *yom* in Genesis.[2]

The Use of Specific Numbers with Day

Some Young Earth Creationists argue that every time the Scriptures use the word *day* with a specific number, it is intended to be understood as a literal twenty-four hours. Therefore, the days in Genesis 1 must also be twenty-four-hour days in a literal week. This reasoning is flawed, however, because context is the most important factor in determining the meaning of a given word or expression. Genesis 1 provides clues to its nonliteral interpretation, and its own context takes precedence over uses of *day* with numbers elsewhere in the Bible. If Genesis 1 intends to use the structure of week for theological purposes, as we have demonstrated, there is only one way to describe a week: adding up seven days.

Similarly flawed reasoning is the argument against a figurative meaning of the word *day* if the word is not used figuratively elsewhere in Genesis. It is possible for a word to be used only once in a particular way in any given document or context. The lone instance does not require another meaning just because it is the only usage with its particular meaning. For example, the Hebrew word 'alluph usually means "close friend" (used seven times this way). But it can also mean "cattle," though it is used only one time this way in the Hebrew Bible (Ps. 144:14).[3] No translator proposes that its use in Psalm 144:14 should mean "close friend" just because that is what it means in all of its other uses. Then the passage would read, in parallel with the previous line (v. 13),

> May our sheep bring forth thousands . . .
> May our close friend be heavy with young . . .

So we reject the specious argument that *because* we don't see the term *day* with a number used figuratively elsewhere in Scripture, *then* it cannot have been used that way in Genesis 1. However, while the Hebrew word for *day* in Genesis 1 could have been meant figuratively, whether it was or not must be argued from the context.

If we assume that Genesis 1 intends regular days for the Hebrew term (and, in fact, we do assume that it refers to regular days), we would still not agree that Genesis 1 requires a six twenty-four-hour-day creation. The issue is not with the specific word *yom* ("day") but with the overall presentation to Israel in their context. We are not arguing for a figurative day or even a long creation day as much as for a generally figurative presentation of the entire week. We understand the whole week as a symbolic presentation. Genesis 1 does not intend to give a literal order of creation events; rather, it begins with how Israel already described creation, without comment, and teaches the reality of Yahweh's place as ultimate creator. The use of a particular word does not require a particular interpretation in Genesis 1, but the whole account must be seen in its whole context.

Repetition of the Evening/Morning, Sunset/Sunrise Formula

The evening and morning formula throughout the first six days of Genesis seems to clinch the requirement for six literal twenty-four-hour days. Can any other kind of day have a sunrise and sunset? Why else would Genesis use this description so consistently? However, there are problems with this conclusion. First, Daniel uses "evening" and "morning" together to refer to days, but they are used figuratively, showing that the phrase does not require a literal interpretation (Dan. 8:14[4]). In addition, the placement of evening before morning is unusual. Rather than summarizing the day, the order seems to lead us to the next day by summarizing the night. This unusual turn of phrase may be a clue that there is more in the text than we initially perceive from our contemporary context. We suggested in chapter 8 that the reference here may actually be aimed as a polemic against the Egyptian understanding of the nighttime battle of the sun god with chaos and his enemies. Genesis challenges this by presenting the night-to-day transition smoothly without conflict, chaos, or question. God is in control and the progress of history goes unquestioningly toward his assured goal of a good creation.

We understand why today's reader naturally thinks of a literal day when reading Genesis 1, and we would assume that the reader in Moses' day probably thought the same thing. A twenty-four-hour day is the only kind of day we know that has an evening and a morning. But even if, for the sake of argument, we were to expand the days to equal millions of years (the "day/age" theory), the theory would still not support an evolutionary scheme—either naturalistic evolution or theistic evolution—because it is impossible to explain how plant life, created on the third day, could have developed and been sustained on the earth before the creation of the sun and moon on the fourth day. The day/age theory is an example of concordism (see chapter 3) that does not take into account the ancient Near Eastern worldview.

If the ancient reader would have naturally thought of a twenty-four-hour day, then how can the passage mean anything other than a recent creation? Let's start with an observation we have already discussed: there were three evenings and mornings before the creation of the sun and moon! While we may naturally think of typical days with evenings and mornings, we do not think of typical days without sun and moon. The progression of the week is a clue that it does not represent our typical kind of day or week (see chapter 4). It was a divine workweek, not a human workweek. God went about his work of creating, taking the evening off (instead of fighting chaos and enemies) and starting again the next day where he left off. He was leading up to the climax, the creation of human life, and then to the completion of his week, his Sabbath rest. Exodus 31:17 points out that God was refreshed by his rest, and that his workweek set a pattern for mankind.

God, however, is not literally bound by time. Nor does he get literally tired. He does not need the evening off to sleep, or a Sabbath to be refreshed. Darkness and light are alike to him (Ps. 139:12). Therefore, the "week" of creation was not for his sake but for mankind's, as the Law later makes clear. Through Moses he framed the creation account in story form so that it would make sense to Israel, especially with its comparisons and contrasts to creation stories from other nations. And he did so in the unique framework of a week, so that we would have a pattern for our own rhythm of life—a rhythm that will continually remind us that we are God's workmanship, that our times are in his hands, and that we are created to worship him. None of the other ancient Near Eastern creation stories is based on a week because they do not order time in this way. The clues within the text help us to understand that the days of Genesis are figurative days that complete a figurative week, in order to give us a real pattern for work and for worship.

Death Before Adam and Eve

Our understanding of Genesis 1 does not require an old earth. In fact we believe that Genesis 1 does not deal with the age of the universe at all, and so the question of the length of time for creation is a separate question to be answered by scientific inquiry. The current state of science indicates an old earth, but of course this can change. The question of whether death occurred before the fall, however, and the biblical teaching on death are still pertinent.

If the earth is old and the creation of humanity in Adam and Eve is relatively recent, then the clear implication is that there was death before Adam and Eve's sin. One alternative suggestion is that the earth is geologically ancient but all biological life is recent. However, the same evidence that points to an old earth—geology and radiometric dating—also points to ancient forms of biological life in fossils. Thus, the data would suggest that there was death before Adam.

The Bible, as early as Genesis 1, seems to clash with the idea that death could have preceded Adam. The creation account states seven times that God looked at his creation and declared it to be good. How could a world of fierce competition for survival and a world where millions of species became extinct be considered good? Further, and more importantly, doesn't the Bible actually say that death began with Adam (e.g., Rom. 5:12–14)? Then, how could there have been death before him? We suggest that careful consideration of the relevant texts offers an answer.

While we do accept the possibility that the earth is very old (the age of the earth is a legitimate scientific field of study) and that the creation of humanity is relatively recent, we are not advocating any particular scientific conclusion. We believe that God may have intervened often in the history of creation to produce exactly the forms of plant and animal life that he wanted on the earth, leading up to the climax of creation, human beings, and we believe that he specifically intervened in the creation of human beings (Adam and Eve). We humans are distinct intellectually and spiritually from all of the rest of God's creation, made "in his image" to represent him on the earth. All of creation is the result of direct, divine Providence.

Understanding Genesis 1 (Gen. 1:1–2:3) symbolically does not also require a figurative understanding of everything in Genesis 2 (Gen. 2:4–25). In fact, Genesis 2 presents a different sort of account, one in which Adam and Eve are the historical ancestors of the human race. The genealogy in Genesis 5:1–5 summarizes the significance of the creation account in relationship to mankind, and it names *Adam* in the same way it subsequently names other historical individuals. Other biblical references to the genealogy (e.g., Luke 3:38), to Adam (Rom. 5:12–21; 1 Cor. 15:22), and to Eve (2 Cor. 11:3) assume that these were real individuals.

This does not mean that the story of their creation and fall in Genesis 2–3 does not include symbolism and figurative language, but it does mean that we believe Genesis is describing historical characters.

If there was physical death in the animal realm before Adam was created, how can the creation account affirm that everything was *good*? This depends on what we mean by *good*. The word has many different meanings, depending on the context. When God says that something is *good*, it means at least that it accomplishes his purposes. For instance, in Genesis 50:20, Joseph speaks to his brothers about their egregious evil against him when they sold him into slavery: "As for you, you meant evil against me, but God meant it for good, to bring it about that many people should be kept alive, as they are today." What appeared to be evil from a human perspective was actually good from God's perspective because it accomplished his sovereign purpose for his covenant people. This text is significant because it frames Genesis in statements about God and goodness; the book began with seven assertions that "God saw that it was good," and it ends with the assessment of a situation that "God meant . . . for good."

This use of *good* at the end of Genesis is similar (though including more direct intention) to the comparison already made between Genesis 1 and the Memphite Theology (see chapter 7, "God Rests"). God rested after creating a well-ordered universe that is functioning properly, much like Ptah, who rested in satisfaction with the cosmos in order. Ancient Egypt (and so also Israel) would not have expected satisfaction with creation to include an absence of death but a harmony and proper working of the cosmos.

Without commenting on the moral nature of animal death, the comparison between Genesis 1 and Genesis 50 suggests that everything, including physical death in the animal world, accomplishes God's sovereign purpose for creation. If God ultimately used the greatest evil (the crucifixion of Christ) to produce the greatest good (the redemption of God's creation), could he not use animal death to accomplish his ultimate good? Can you imagine a world in which there was no death? How long would it be before bacteria or viruses had overwhelmed the world? Or fruit flies or mosquitoes? Or snakes or dinosaurs? Death is a daily part of God's beneficence to us today. It was also part of preparing the earth for man's habitation: we'd be unlikely to have oil reserves today if it hadn't been for the death of plants and animals in our geological history.[5]

But doesn't Scripture say that there was no death until Adam's sin? Actually, it doesn't, although many have interpreted it to mean that. God did tell Adam that if he rebelled against the Lord's kingship by eating of the forbidden fruit, then "in the day that you eat of it you shall surely die" (Gen. 2:17). God said only that *mankind* would die, not that anything else would. But, in fact, Adam did not die physically *on that day*—at least, not if one takes "day" to be a twenty-four-hour period in Genesis 3. He and Eve both lived long lives and had children after their sin. They did die eventually, but would they have lived immortally if they had not sinned? We think not, agreeing with Kenneth Mathews:

> There is no suggestion from the passage, as is assumed by some, that Adam was created immortal but subsequently forfeited immortality by his sin. There is a difference between man's creation, in which he receives life by the divine inbreathing (2:7), and the perpetuation of that life gained by appropriating the tree of life (cf. 3:22). Immortality is the trait of deity alone.[6]

In other words, people were created with a clear choice but without any clear predisposition as to which choice they would make. The text does not say what would have happened if Adam had simply walked away from both the Tree of Life and the Tree of the Knowledge of Good and Evil and decided to eat from neither! Would he and Eve have died physically? That is entirely possible. Consider Genesis 3:22: God did say that he must cut them off from the Tree of Life lest they eat and live forever. Since eating from the Tree of the Knowledge of Good and Evil brought the immediate result of knowing good and evil, we would assume that eating from the Tree of Life would have brought the immediate result of "life," whatever that was intended to mean. Judging from God's explanation, it included living "forever." So perhaps the passage is indicating that if they did not eat from the Tree of Life, they would physically die. They had to make a choice to eat or not to eat in order to determine if they would live or die. The consequences of sin included ultimate, though not immediate, physical death. Assuming that the passage is intended to be literal, if they had then eaten of the Tree of Life, would they then have countered that physical consequence of sin and been stuck forever in a sinful physical existence?[7]

What we do clearly know is that God presented a choice to humankind (Adam and Eve), life or death. The same choice is reiterated to Israel in Deuteronomy 30. Obedience to the word of God meant life, but disobedience meant death (vv. 15–20). Specifically, Genesis 2 presents immortality as a consequence of eating from the Tree of Life and death as the consequence of eating from the Tree of the Knowledge of Good and Evil. Man did not have a certain future until he chose life or death! This means that there was not yet any physical death for mankind prior to the fall (we are affirming a historical Adam and Eve). It does not mean, however, that Adam and Eve did not know from other creatures what death was.

As a result of their sin, God cut Adam and Eve off from the Tree of Life, so they would necessarily die physically—eventually. Physical death "spread to all men" (Rom. 5:12) because we have all been cut off from the Tree of Life that was in the garden. As a result of their sin, Adam and Eve died a spiritual death on "that day." They were separated from God, their source of spiritual life. Spiritual death has spread to all mankind because of Adam's sin and our participation in it.

A key phrase relevant to our study of Genesis 1 is "and so death spread *to all men*" (Rom. 5:12, emphasis added). This effect did not include the animal world, because (1) animals were not given moral responsibility before God, (2) they do not experience spiritual life, and (3) they (presumably) will not experience eternal life. John Murray is to the point:

"When [Paul] says 'entered into the world' he refers to the beginning of sin in the human race and 'the world' means the sphere of human existence."[8]

First Corinthians 15 follows this theme to its redemptive conclusion. Death entered the human race through Adam but life comes through Jesus (1 Cor. 15:21–22). This ultimate life does not come from returning to the Tree of Life in a sinful state. Instead, we must have the atonement that cleanses from sin and the life that Jesus, our atoning sacrifice, secured with his resurrection. Not only does Christ reverse the curse of sin and death, but he also will provide mankind with new and eternal spiritual bodies that can fully participate in the new life (1 Cor. 15:35–49). This transformation will include a full expression of the image of God (Christ) in a new and glorious way (v. 49).

Paul's description of life and death does not deal with the animal kingdom. The whole context is man, sin, and death, in contrast to Christ, victory, life, and ultimate rule. The final state is not merely a return to Eden. In fact, Paul clearly says that "flesh and blood cannot inherit the kingdom of God" (1 Cor. 15:50). While he could be speaking figuratively, he nonetheless makes a significant point that the new bodies are spiritual and very different—as different as the flower is from the seed. It would seem that Christ does not take mankind back to a pre-fall state but ahead to a much greater and more glorious transformed and heavenly state. The abolishment of death as the last enemy (v. 26) refers to the ultimate life given to all those in Christ. It does not tell us that animals will live forever, nor does it tell us that before the fall there was no death in the animal kingdom. Paul simply does not address these issues.

It is not a biblical problem, then, for animal death to have preceded Adam's fall. The Bible does not speak directly to whether animals died before Adam's fall, but it does say clearly that the result of Adam's sin affected humanity. Perhaps God's threat of judgment assumed that Adam had seen death. How could Adam have known what death was and that it was to be feared? Wouldn't he have asked, "What does 'surely die' mean?"

The Curse on Creation

The New Testament has a reference to God's judgment on creation after the fall in Romans 8:20–21: "For the creation was subjected to futility, not willingly, but because of him who subjected it, in hope that the creation itself will be set free from its bondage to corruption and obtain the freedom of the glory of the children of God." While the apostle Paul seems to refer to Genesis 3:17–19, some Young Earth expositors interpret this statement to mean that there was no death before God's curse and perhaps even the laws of physics (such as entropy) changed.[9] But is that really what this passage means?

Most New Testament scholars agree that Romans 8 refers to the judgment of Genesis 3. And most would agree that something changed after the curse. But the text does not necessarily mean that there was no death before the curse. The reference to creation in Romans is not to humans but to the earth—affecting plant life and probably also animal life.[10] This is clearly in keeping with the curse in Genesis:

> Cursed is the ground because of you;
> in pain you shall eat of it all the days of your life;
> thorns and thistles it shall bring forth for you;
> and you shall eat the plants of the field. (Gen. 3:17–18)

The curse is focused on the plant world, but the text does not say that this is the beginning of the death of plants. Rather, it introduces a change in the relationship of Adam to his task of farming from this point; now his labor will be complicated and frustrated by thorns and thistles. As Paul stated it, creation was "subjected to futility." In the terms of Genesis, things are no longer "good." The ground is no longer able simply to serve its purpose unimpeded. This does not require a wholesale change in physics (or a new creation of pesky plants) but an inability to be what it was designed to be by not easily producing for its (fallen) ruler. The Greek term translated "futility" is the same one used in the Greek translation of Ecclesiastes to describe Solomon's perspective on the meaninglessness of life under the sun in and of itself, usually translated "vanity." As Cranfield aptly states, "We may think of the whole magnificent theatre of the universe together with all its splendid properties and all the chorus of sub-human life, created to glorify God but unable to do so fully, so long as man, the chief actor in the drama of God's praise, fails to contribute his rational part."[11]

In conclusion, we do not believe that Scripture *requires* the belief that creation is a recent event, accomplished in six literal twenty-four-hour days; nor do we believe that there was no death before the sin of Adam and Eve. Those who do interpret Genesis 1 in this way are attempting to be faithful to the text of Scripture as they understand it, to uphold its utter trustworthiness as God's revelation. But we believe their interpretation is influenced more by a modern worldview than an ancient Near Eastern worldview.

Chapter Fourteen

TOWARD A CREATION THEOLOGY

"In the beginning, God ..."

The stark clarity and profound simplicity of this simple beginning to the Christian and Jewish Scriptures capture the imagination and hearts of believers. It is the beginning of the story of God's cosmos and of our world. It is the ultimate first principle from which all law(s) derives. It is the necessary reality to which we cling in hope of eternal life. He was there at the beginning, he will be there at the end, and everything in between is under his ultimate authority. The Word of God and the world of God reveal his power and his majesty. The apostle Paul trumpeted this truth in Romans 1:20:

> For his invisible attributes, namely, his eternal power and divine nature, have been clearly perceived, ever since the creation of the world, in the things that have been made.

Paul may have been echoing David's praise from Psalm 19:1:

> The heavens declare the glory of God,
> and the sky above proclaims his handiwork.

With our biblical background, when we ponder creation we are led to marvel in the greatness of God.

But what about those with no biblical background? What about people from pagan cultures who, from their earliest days, have been taught that there are *gods*, not God; that creation is itself divine; and that religious rituals are necessary to harness the forces of nature and to keep the gods appeased? These people need a completely new worldview. They need to start over and to relearn the story of beginnings. They need to meet the God of the Bible in his works and in his Word so they can understand the story of history from God's perspective. They need a new starting point so they can arrive at the correct finishing point.

This is what we believe is happening in Genesis 1. We believe that Israel, having spent four centuries in Egypt, was immersed in the worldview of the Egyptians. This does not mean that the Israelites had no exposure to the God of Abraham, but they certainly knew the gods of the Egyptians. Abraham himself had come from a pagan Mesopotamian background, and his own understanding of creation may have been confused.

The ten plagues defeated the gods of Egypt. The miracles of the exodus introduced Yahweh as the unrivaled God of Israel. Now as Israel waited in the wilderness, perhaps at Sinai, they needed to relearn the story of creation from the perspective of their God so that they would

"The heavens declare the glory of God, and the sky above proclaims his handiwork" (Psalm 19:1). (Photo credit: Jeanne Miller)

be equipped with truth to accept God's covenant and to trust and obey him as they prepared to conquer the land of Canaan. The revelation of Genesis 1 cleared up any errors regarding who was the creator, and it gave the people a theology of creation in terms they could understand.

What did Genesis 1:1–2:4 mean to Israel in the second millennium before Christ? Let's begin by looking at a summary of the creation narrative, to read it as the original readers may have heard it.

The Significance of the Days of Creation

God sets about his divine workweek, preparing the stage for mankind and for his relationship with mankind. He fills the stage with all forms of life and beauty, goodness that can come only from him. Moses underscores the amazing details that are significant about and unique to the earth in relation to the rest of the universe, evidencing the careful design that went into making the earth compatible for life. Genesis 1, then, offers the biblical theology behind the "anthropic principle," which suggests that the nature of the universe must be consistent with the ability of life as we know it to exist, even requiring intelligent life and implying design.

On day 1, God separates light from darkness and puts day and night into motion. This is the necessary starting point for all that is to follow, bringing light and order to the infinite disordered mass of water. He shows himself to be the source and controller of day and night. Light is not divine (sun or moon), and darkness is not a threat. Out of the chaos of the watery mass, God first produces order, teaching that darkness is not to be feared and light is not to be revered. God himself is the creator of light, both spiritual and physical. Significantly, Genesis ends with God bringing good out of the desolation and darkness in Joseph's life, bringing light and life to people (Gen. 50:20).

On day 2, God orders the firmament into place to hold back the threatening waters above and below. He is the one who keeps the world in place and prepares the stage where mankind will act out the history of God's kingdom. God holds back the waters and then releases them according to his will.

On day 3, God orders the waters into one place and commands dry land to appear. On the land he calls into being living plants, which will nourish mankind. He founds the earth upon the waters, establishing his authority over both land and water. He provides food for the creatures he will soon create. The stage is fully set. All that was formerly *tohu* (desolate) is now arranged and in order. Everything wet and everything dry belongs to God. He can do with it what he wants.

On day 4, God begins to decorate the cosmos, putting the heavenly lights into place. The lights, deliberately left unnamed, serve as impersonal markers of time. They are not deified as controllers of history as in other cultures. They do not control the affairs of mankind or the movements of history because only God can do that.

On day 5, God orders into life the living creatures that fill the heretofore empty sky and waters. Every niche of creation has its purpose and its inhabitants. None of it just happened. What is more, none rivals God's power or authority. Even the great sea creatures—the feared "monsters"—are simply creatures under the authority of God.

On day 6, God fills the last empty niche of his creation—earth. First, he makes the animals, "all creatures great and small." Then he fashions the unique creature, made in the image of God himself—mankind. This is the climax of the creative process: human beings made in God's image to serve as his regents on the earth. All creatures made before humans are under humanity's delegated authority. All that was *bohu* (empty) now teems with life.

On day 7, the divine workweek is complete, never to be repeated. God has finished ordering and filling his cosmos, and he has put on the earth one to look after his interests and to bring him proper worship and glory. It is time for God to put away his workman's garb, don his royal robes, and take his throne to rest. And it is time for this new creation to join him in that repose and to enjoy the marvels and beauty of creation in a family relationship with the Creator. It is an endless day, with the offer of unlimited fellowship to all who desire it.

How does this retelling of the story impact the theology of the original readers in their setting? What difference does it make in light of their world—and, eventually, of ours?

Genesis 1 Billboards the Goodness of God

If we see nothing else from Genesis 1, we must see that God's creation shouts that he is good. The sevenfold repetition of God's good evaluation, climaxing in the creation of man as "very good," highlights God's eternal intent to bring good out of the darkness (just as we recognized in Joseph's words [Gen. 50:20]). This goodness is the result of God's nature, and it is constantly celebrated in the hymnology of Israel as God delivers his people and brings justice to his creation to demonstrate his good sovereign power as Creator and King (1 Chron. 16:34; Pss. 34:8; 100:5; 106:1; 107:1; 118:1, 29; 135:3; 136:1; 145:9). Even in a fallen world, we see beauty in nature that awes us; we experience occasional outbursts of joy that can only be hints of heaven; we give and receive love that is transcendent and transformational. We who know and trust God believe that this is a reflection of his purpose for creation—that his goodness would be made known.

In Exodus 33:19 God promises that he will allow Moses to see and experience his goodness. Then, as Exodus 34:6–7 expounds it, he parades that goodness and describes it: mercy, grace, patience, love, faithfulness, forgiveness, and justice. On the other hand, death, disease, fractured relationships, and all sorts of suffering in our world cry out for relief. From the beginning God has always been willing to use all of that suffering for ultimate good and for his glory in his kingdom plan. While we recognize the tension created by the possibility of death before sin in God's good creation, we also believe that the ultimate goal of God's good creation is the elimination of both sin and death (1 Cor. 15:50–56). So even in the face of suffering, God's goodness is celebrated in his preservation of life and ultimate deliverance of his people from their suffering and pain (Pss. 86:5–7; 107), which is only finally understood in the context of worship.

Know that the LORD, he is God!
It is he who made us, and we are his;
we are his people, and the sheep of his pasture.
Enter his gates with thanksgiving,
and his courts with praise!
Give thanks to him; bless his name!
For the LORD is good;
his steadfast love endures forever,
and his faithfulness to all generations. (Ps. 100:3–5)

Genesis 1 Depersonalizes Creation

Creation is the product of the will and word of God. He existed before it, and he brought it into existence by separating out each of the functions so that all of creation would accomplish his purpose. It is not composed of the divided body of a goddess. It has no life of its own; it has never had a life of its own. It is an *it*, not a *he* or a *she*. Therefore it deserves no reverence, no worship.

How important was this fact? How important *is* this fact? In a climate of paganism, the world seems to breathe with a life of its own. This ancient air is recaptured in part by the Mother Earth resurgence of our own era, a return to pagan influences. It is also recaptured in part by the recent movement toward Eastern mysticism under the influence of Hinduism, which teaches that everything is god. In paganism God is viewed as part of the world and, as such, he is subject to the influences of the world.

This was the spiritual climate in ancient Egypt. And perhaps, apart from the knowledge of Yahweh, it is understandable. Humans were virtually helpless against the forces of nature. They understood none of the "scientific" explanations for weather, for the rising and setting of the sun, for the seasons. Their creation stories and religious myths brought nature to life.

Genesis 1 counters this pagan system. It depersonalizes nature, putting it in its place and raising God to his place. The cosmos has no will of its own but is subject to the will of Yahweh. The writer of Hebrews understood the creation account in this way: "By faith we understand that the universe was created by the word of God, so that what is seen was not made out of things that are visible" (Heb. 11:3).

Genesis 1 Dethrones the Gods of Paganism

By depersonalizing the creation, Genesis 1 dethrones the gods of paganism and elevates Yahweh alone to the cosmic throne. Egypt, Canaan, and Mesopotamia were awash with gods, some major and some minor. In some cases their gods were like humans at their worst—selfish, greedy, rapacious, lustful. They were the projections of humans who created their gods in their own image. Humans were made to feed them and appease them, in hopes that they would earn the gods' good favor and thus be cared for themselves. There were no atheists in the ancient Near East; the gods influenced every part of life.

Imagine what it would have been like to go outside at night to peer at the ancient heavens: without electricity, without ambient lighting, the stars tease you into trying to touch them. Their shimmering makes them dance to life. They rule that inky blackness. But then the sun emerges from his nighttime journey, where he has made his way through the darkness back to where he began on all the previous days. With victorious might, he chases the stars away.

Genesis 1 dethrones these gods. They are merely lights: the greater light and the lesser lights. They are not gods. They are billboards for seasons, and they are separators of light and darkness. And they don't even appear until the middle of God's creative week. He doesn't need them; they need him. God is the creator of everything that exists. Nothing existed before him, and nothing exists without his decree. He has no rivals for his throne. This is his proclamation in Isaiah 45:6–7:

That people may know, from the rising of the sun
and from the west, that there is none besides me;

I am the LORD, and there is no other.
I form light and create darkness,
I make well-being and create calamity,
I am the LORD, who does all these things.

Genesis 1 Establishes Order in the Cosmos

In Egypt the setting sun was the sign that a god had left his post. Darkness was for them a return to primordial chaos. Without the sun's reign, the world was full of danger.

But not for the people of God. God created both light *and* darkness.

He made the moon to mark the seasons;
the sun knows its time for setting.
You make darkness, and it is night,
when all the beasts for the forest creep about.
The young lions roar for their prey,
seeking their food from God.
When the sun rises, they steal away
and lie down in their dens. (Ps. 104:19–22)

In fact, God named the darkness *night* (Gen. 1:5). To give something a name was to exercise authority over it. Darkness is under God's control. Once God began to bring order to the original creation, it was all under his control from the first day. The people of God had nothing to fear from the darkness:

If I say, "Surely the darkness shall cover me,
and the light about me be night,"
even the darkness is not dark to you;
the night is bright as the day,
for darkness is as light with you. (Ps. 139:11–12)

Genesis 1 Fills the Void

At its beginning the earth was "desolate and empty."[1] God filled the emptiness out of his own creative energy and to fulfill his own creative purpose. Each step of the creation was "good," accomplishing exactly the purpose he had for it. Nothing was left to chance; there were no un-filled niches. The mind of Yahweh providentially guided the preparation of the earth for the climax of creation: the man and woman. The psalm-ist captures this awesome reality:

> O LORD, how manifold are your works!
> In wisdom have you made them all;
> the earth is full of your creatures....
> When you send forth your Spirit, they are created,
> and you renew the face of the ground. (Ps. 104:24, 30)

Genesis 1 Establishes Mankind as God's Vice-Regent

The immensity of the universe makes us feel dwarfed and insignifi-cant. It humbles us and prompts us to ponder our purpose for existing. The words of the psalmist echo our thoughts:

> When I look at your heavens, the work of your fingers,
> the moon and the stars, which you have set in place,
> what is man that you are mindful of him,
> and the son of man that you care for him? (Ps. 8:3–4)

Our minds work like the psalmist's mind: Who are we? Why would God care for us?

The answer is a surprise in the ancient world. Mankind, collectively and individually, was not created to wait hand and foot on the deities. We were not created by lazy, gluttonous gods, who look to us to house and feed them. Instead, we were created in God's own image to partner with him in establishing his reign over all the earth to his glory. "Fill the earth" and "have dominion," he said to the first humans (Gen. 1:28).

The psalmist understood this:

> Yet you have made him a little lower than the heavenly beings
> and crowned him with glory and honor.
> You have given him dominion over the works of your hands;
> you have put all things under his feet,
> all sheep and oxen,
> and also the beasts of the field,
> the birds of the heavens, and the fish of the sea,
> whatever passes along the paths of the seas. (Ps. 8:5–8)

What the image of God consists of is demonstrated further in Genesis 2, the study of which is beyond the scope of this book.[2] In short, in their physical being, people are related to the earth because they are made from dust (Gen. 2:7). They are not divine because no part of any god is used in their creation. What makes them different is, first, God's declaration of their higher status and purpose, and then his direct impartation of his own Spirit, the breath (ruach, "Spirit") of life. The creation of mankind was distinct, and people were empowered and authorized to represent God as regents over the earth.

Such truth would have energized Israel when they exited Egypt. Individually, each Israelite was no different from any other human being; they were not physically different from the pagans. But because of their covenant relationship with Creator God, they were heirs of his appointment to be a nation of kings and priests, to establish his rightful reign first over the land that he offered them and then, through their service and worship of him,[3] over all of the earth. As Psalm 8 shows, even the effects of sin do not cancel God's creation mandate for mankind.

Genesis 1 Invites Mankind to Worship and Rest

When mankind arrived on the scene in Genesis 1, the work of creation was completed. God did it all, all by himself. The very first thing for people to do was to join God in his rest. By contrast, the gods of

Egypt and Mesopotamia enslaved and overworked men so that the gods could rest. But not the God of Israel:

> For he knows our frame;
> he remembers that we are dust. (Ps. 103:14)

If John Walton's theory that the creation week intends to lead up to the enthronement of God in his cosmic temple is correct,[4] then people arrive just in time to experience and celebrate God's enthronement. God did not need man's help to build his temple. In fact, man had nothing to offer. Neither did God need man's sacrifices for food. He is not dependent upon mankind in any way.

Even if Walton is incorrect, one lesson remains unchanged: God inaugurates human life by offering mankind the privilege of joining in his rest, of starting life by completely depending upon God to provide all that is necessary for life and godliness. Life begins with God. Our finite productivity emanates from his unlimited supply. Life with God precedes service for God. Trust yields obedience. Obedience leads to rest.

The writer of Hebrews appears to have understood this perfectly, both as it related to the life of Israel and as it relates to our lives. Israel failed to trust and obey God in its wilderness wanderings, and therefore the people were unable to experience rest, which in Moses' and Joshua's time would have been the conquest of Canaan and spiritual dominance of the land (Heb. 3–4). Likewise, if we fail to trust and obey, we will never experience God's purpose for our lives (Heb. 3:12–15).

Genesis 1 Completes the Process of Creation

No other ancient Near Eastern creation story includes a week of creation. It is this unique feature in the biblical account that has resulted in strong conflict over the scientific implications of Genesis 1. We have tried to demonstrate why we do not believe the week needs to be taken literally as seven twenty-four-hour days. But, as we've said, if the week is not literal, why refer to it at all? We propose three main reasons.

First, this is another feature in the biblical story that sets it apart from the other accounts. It taught the people of God that there was a distinctive rhythm to their life, a rhythm that climaxed (or began) each week with a withdrawal from the normal duties of life in order to fellowship with and worship their God, the God of creation and the God of the exodus. Their weekly practice of entering into his rest provided a tangible demonstration of their submission to the rule of God (Exod. 31:12–17). Rest was built into the meaning of creation.

Second, the week taught that there was process to creation—that it didn't happen all on one day. What purpose does that serve? The process led to a climax, the creation of mankind. In order to heighten the climax, there had to be process. If creation were envisioned as happening all at once, there would have been no climax to the story. If it all occurred on one day, there would need to be an hour-by-hour elaboration to build to a climax. (And that structure might well have led to arguments over whether the account meant one literal twenty-four-hour day!)

Third, the framework of the week taught that there was an end to creating, and thus that history was not a cyclical struggle. The Egyptians of Moses' time saw creation happening anew each day with the rising of the sun. Other pagans saw creation being renewed with the return of the rainy season and the new growth of vegetation. But the God of Israel effortlessly finished his creating and then rested with an unending rest from his work of cosmic creation.

This is another way of saying that God set history on a trajectory with an end in sight. Time is not endless cycles but is progressing toward the goal of creation itself—that the earth might be filled with the glory of God.

Genesis 1 Claims All Glory for Yahweh

There is only one Creator God. In Genesis 1, it is *Elohim*. In Genesis 2, he is also identified as *Yahweh*. But it is the same God, *Yahweh Elohim*. He is the God of Israel.

All other gods are pretenders. There is a great paean of praise to this God in the prophecy of Isaiah:

Do you not know? Do you not hear?
Has it not been told you from the beginning?
Have you not understood from the foundations of the earth?
It is he who sits above the circle of the earth,
and its inhabitants are like grasshoppers;
who stretches out the heavens like a curtain,
and spreads them like a tent to dwell in;
who brings princes to nothing
and makes the rulers of the earth as emptiness. (Isa. 40:21–23)

The Tablet of Shamash shows the sun god (Shamash) on his throne in heaven over the cosmic waters (above the sky), but if Yahweh created all this, Shamash is a pretender—merely a "greater light" in the sky. (Photo credit: Kim Walton, courtesy of the British Museum)

Earlier in the same chapter, the prophet had cried out, "Behold your God!" (Isa. 40:9). And when people looked to where his finger was pointing, they saw a shepherd (Isa. 40:11). This is the same God who proclaims:

> Before me no god was formed,
> nor shall there be any after me.
> I, I am the LORD,
> And besides me there is no savior. (Isa. 43:10–11)

> Turn to me and be saved,
> all the ends of the earth!
> For I am God, and there is no other. (Isa. 45:22)

Above all, the Genesis 1 creation account eliminates all the greater and lesser gods of all the nations of the world, both then and now. It eliminates fear of all the territorial gods of pagan ancient Near Eastern religions. It eliminates the fearful superstitious questioning as to whether we might have overlooked some god or something divine. It establishes the God of Israel alone as God, and serves to bring him all of the honor for creating and caring:

> I am the LORD; that is my name;
> my glory I give to no other,
> nor my praise to carved idols. (Isa. 42:8)

Chapter Fifteen

THE END OF DEBATE?

W e wish that we could offer the final word on the debate over the meaning of Genesis 1, but we realize this is probably impossible. In fact, we anticipate that our work will be critiqued, evaluated, corrected, attacked, and (hopefully) even praised by some. It will probably need revising in a few years as more information becomes available and as our perspective is highlighted or adjusted by subsequent debate. In other words, this work is just part of an ongoing discussion that probably won't end until heaven.

In the meantime, we hope and pray that for some we have moved the center of the discussion regarding Genesis 1 away from what one believes about science to what the Scriptures say and mean. If we are right in our approach to Genesis 1—that is, reading it from the perspective of ancient Near Eastern religious context—then the issue is not scientific but theological. If Genesis 1 seems like a fairy tale to naturalist scientists today, the world of physics would have seemed like a fairy tale to the original readers of Genesis 1. But both would have been wrong, because the theological truths of Genesis 1 provide as much of a framework of reality as does scientific discovery.

God could have revealed science in 1200 b.c., or in 4000 b.c., or at any other point in biblical history. It would have been accurate science, even if the people did not understand it. But the original readers would have approached the Scriptures with as much puzzlement as do the majority of today's scientists who (wrongly) believe that the Bible intends to reflect the scientific origins of the universe. To make Genesis work scientifically, few imagine that it can be taken literally. Yet many within the body of Christ are pressured to believe that Genesis 1 is scientifically accurate as written and their spirituality is called into question if they do not agree.

In his own study, Johnny had occasion to correspond by email with a top-notch geneticist who retired from Cornell University. He had been an atheist most of his life, and said that even after becoming a Christian, for a long time he remained a "compromised" Christian and a theistic evolutionist. He wrote:

> I am now a creationist. I am getting stronger and stronger scientific reasons to defend my position, but these are not the real basis of my faith. As I have studied Scripture I have seen that believing God is "counted as righteousness," and that unbelief really is sin. Salvation comes from surrendering: 1) our will, 2) our heart, and 3) our mind to the Lord. Have you done step 3? Would you be willing to be a fool for Christ?[1]

This brilliant, well-educated brother in Christ knows more about science than we will ever begin to know. And it is obvious that when he became a Christian, his mind was renewed. But he implies that reading Genesis 1 as science is equivalent to believing God for salvation and that anyone who does not read it this way is actually compromising his or her faith. If Genesis 1 is intended to be read as science, then it does need to be understood that way. If it is not intended to be read as science, then it is *misreading* it to understand it that way. The assumption that Genesis 1 is science is what we hope to lay to rest with this book, so that we can learn from Genesis what God meant to teach through Moses. We believe that there are exegetical, contextual reasons to believe that Genesis 1 was not intended to teach a scientific view of creation.

In critique of our own work, we believe our greatest strength is in helping laypeople and students ask the most vital interpretive question that needs to be asked in the study of any portion of Scripture: What did the original author (and Author) mean for the original readers? In this case, what did (God's Spirit through) Moses mean for the Israelites as they came out of Egypt? This question must precede any discussion of scientific implications. We hope that we have been able to help our readers move mentally and spiritually back through time to the second millennium B.C. and get a grasp on what the issues were for the Israelites as they pondered the creation and Creator and as they worked through the misinformation of religious myths from Egypt, Mesopotamia, and Canaan. We must remember that Scripture was written in different languages from ours; this automatically means that the culture was also different. Complicating the issues of interpretation is also the fact that it was written long before our time. If we ignore these facts, we are in danger of reading into the Bible error instead of reading from the Bible truth.

We hope that no one will misunderstand our words and read into this book something that is not here. As we said earlier, we are trying to accommodate neither Darwinism nor science. Naturalistic Darwinism is incompatible with the Creator God of the Bible, who knows nothing of chance; and Genesis 1 neither intends to answer nor speaks to scientific questions. Rather, the exegetical questions, including context, are the concerns that we must evaluate.

We pray that readers will see that we are two people who love God deeply and revere his Word profoundly. We will believe whatever the Scriptures mandate, but we want to make sure that what we believe is actually what Scripture means because that is how we bring the greatest glory to God. We pray that you have this same commitment. And if, in the process of coming to fuller understanding, we happen to disagree, we will honor one another as true-hearted followers of the Lord Jesus Christ.

NOTES

Chapter 1: Asking the Right Question

1. Whitcomb and Morris, *The Genesis Flood.*
2. For one historical perspective on the source and influence of their work, see Numbers, *The Creationists.* He traces the roots of modern creationism to the influence of Seventh-day Adventist George McReady Price on Henry Morris: "It was not until the creationist renaissance of the 1960s, marked by the publication of Whitcomb and Morris's *Genesis Flood* and the subsequent birth of the Creation Research Society, that fundamentalists in large numbers began to read Genesis in the Pricean manner and to equate his views with the intended message of Moses" (p. 8).
3. When I told one of my friends, a PhD in geology from Johns Hopkins University, about my change in thinking based on what I had discovered in Scripture, he said, "I am so thankful to hear you say that. I have believed in the absolute truthfulness of Scripture all my life, and yet knew that what I discovered in geology was true as well. I knew there had to be some other interpretation of Scripture. I've seen so many young students lose their faith because they couldn't put together the Bible and science."
4. We recognize there are differing views on the authorship of Genesis and different understandings of the degree to which Moses composed the initial work, but we believe that he was the substantive author of the text, for which he used sources, and which later was edited. For further discussion, see chapter 5, particularly note 1.

5. Numbers, *Creationists*, 13.

Chapter 2: We've Been Here Before

1. The pre-Reformation Roman Catholic Church based its authority on a combination of church tradition, including papal authority and biblical revelation. However, there is no reason to believe that the Reformation altered the current understanding of the relevant Scriptures that appeared to touch on cosmology. In other words, these interpretations were not unique to the Roman Church.

2. Hummel, *Galileo Connection*, 70.

3. Rowland, *Galileo's Mistake*, 248–49.

4. The Council of Trent, at its fourth session on April 8, 1546, reserved all authority for Bible interpretation for the unanimous consent of the church fathers.

5. "Aristotle's argument for God's existence from the observed fact of motion was to become the foundation of Christian theology in the Middle Ages" (Rowland, *Galileo's Mistake*, 77).

6. See, for example, http://en.wikipedia.org/wiki/Modern_geocentrism for an introduction to the Tychonian Society.

7. See http://www.religionnewsblog.com/13644/dna-tests-contradict-mormon-scripture. A Mormon response can be found at http://www.mormonwiki.com/Book_of_Mormon_DNA.

Chapter 3: Finding Meaning in Genesis 1 (Part 1)

1. Galilei, "Letter to the Grand Duchess."

2. Ibid.

3. Bailey, *Poet and Peasant*, 181.

4. Ross, *Matter of Days*, 144. John Hartnet, on the other hand, argues from this same verse that the universe was literally stretched out by God on day 4 of creation, accounting for the appearance of age and the distances of stars (*Starlight, Time and the New Physics*, 92–105).

5. Hummel, *Galileo Connection*, 27.

6. Ross, *Matter of Days*; cf. also Snoke, *Biblical Case for an Old Earth*.

7. Morris, *Scientific Creationism*, 209–10.

8. Young Earth Creationists are aware of these issues and attempt to respond to them. Cf. Humphreys, *Starlight and Time* and Hartnet, *Starlight, Time and the New Physics*.

9. Ross, *Matter of Days*, 206; cf. also page 86, notes 96, 97. According to Ross the same question was posed by John Lewis, host of *Bible on the Line* radio program, over a period of five years (1987–1993), and the answer was always the same—no.

10. Ibid., 235–36.

Chapter 4: Finding Meaning in Genesis 1 (Part 2)

1. For a discussion of the ancients' concept of the world, including the Hebrew viewpoint, see Walton, *Ancient Near Eastern Thought*, 165–78, and Wright, "Biblical Versus Israelite Images." We cannot be sure what they believed, but we do know how they expressed their views. We assume that much of what they said reflected how they thought about the cosmos, but at least some of them probably did realize that it was not entirely accurate. Many would realize that the sky was not supported on the mountains, at least not the near mountains, and that the rain came from clouds (but did they know how it got in the clouds?).

2. Howard, *Joshua*, 247.

3. Ibid., 249.

4. Unfortunately the attempt to "prove" Joshua's long day has resulted in many variations of urban myth claiming that NASA or some other scientific group has discovered the missing time.

5. Collins, *Language of God*. Collins argues throughout the book that the genome project proves evolution; he summarizes his conclusion on pages 135–42, applies it to Genesis in chapter 6 (pp. 145–48), and addresses Young Earth Creationism in chapter 8 (pp. 171–79).

6. Boyd and Eddy, *Across the Spectrum*, 74. This comment does not necessarily reflect Boyd and Eddy's perspective. Their book presents issues in evangelical theology and the arguments for different views.

7. Sarna, *Genesis*, 3.

8. Emphasis added. This is also the translation of the *Tanakh* (Philadelphia: Jewish Publication Society, 1999).

9. The exception is the date formulas in which the word for "one" is consistently used for days. This is not a date formula, however, even if it refers to days.

10. It only appears ten times and only one other time (Ezra 10:17) is it translated "the first day." In Ezra it is part of a date formula that has unique uses for *'eHad*, the Hebrew word for "one." The use in Genesis 1 is unique. "The indefinite noun plus אחד has a definite sense in the opening chapter of Genesis: יוֹם אֶחָד 'the first day' (Gen. 1:5); this pattern is found nowhere else—even the rest of the account uses indefinite nouns with ordinal numbers (Gen. 1:8, 13, etc.)," Waltke and O'Connor, *Introduction to Biblical Hebrew Syntax*, 274. While this sense may be understood to be definite because of the list it begins, the normal translation of this construction would be "one day" (for example, Gen. 27:45; 33:13) or it could be a specific indefinite, "a certain day" (ibid., 251, sec. 13.8.a). The point is that this is a very unusual way to enumerate a list and leaves several other options open to the Hebrew reader. If the author had intended this list to be a simple listing of days, it seems doubtful he would have done it this way.

11. The only other possible exception is found in Nehemiah 6:5, which is generally translated as definite (see the ESV, NIV, NRSV, KJV, etc.) but need not be definite. It actually makes great sense as an indefinite; after trying to intimidate Nehemiah four times (v. 4), Sanballat and Tobiah tried "a fifth time" with an open letter.

12. While two of these uses provide the article on the number and not the day (1:31, 2:3—contrary to normal attributive adjective use), the disagreement is not unusual for numbered phrases (Walkte and O'Connor, *Introduction to Biblical Hebrew Syntax*, 260).

13. Waltke and Fredricks, *Genesis*, 62. Cf. Sterchi, "Does Genesis 1 Provide a Chronological Sequence?"

14. Sailhamer offers a pair of suggestions why day 1 did not have a definite article, but he ignores the question for days 2–5 (*Genesis*, 28).

15. See Wenham's discussion of these and other connections in the days (*Genesis 1–15*, 6–7).

16. Hugh Ross argues, instead, that the sun was created at the beginning of the week, but made to appear on the fourth day (*Matter of Days*, 78).

17. *naphash*: "to catch your breath, breathe freely." The *Hebrew and Aramaic Lexicon of the Old Testament* defines the usage in the Niphal (this passage) as "to breathe freely, recover" (Koehler et al., 711).

18. Longman, *How to Read Genesis*, 104.

Chapter 5: The Purpose of Genesis

1. This assumption does not preclude a later editing but assumes a real Moses writing to a real Israel coming out of Egypt sometime in the second millennium B.C. We recognize that the original author may have used sources (including perhaps "the book of the generations of Adam," Gen. 5:1). We also recognize that the document must have been edited to some degree after the death of Moses ("Chaldeans" show up after Moses [Gen. 11:28, etc.]; Dan was not called Dan until after Moses [Gen. 14:14]). We are simply affirming as reliable an understanding of the text based on a real Moses who presented a real Israel with the Law and, to a great extent, the Pentateuch that we now know. For discussion on this problem, see Longman, *How to Read Genesis*, 43–58; Garrett, *Rethinking Genesis*.

2. Genesis 5:1 refers to a "book [*sepher*] of the generations of Adam," which Waltke suggests could indicate that Moses used written sources (Waltke and Fredricks, *Genesis*, 113). Cassuto merely suggests it could be referring to the section that follows (*Commentary on the Book of Genesis*, 273).

3. Longman, *How to Read Genesis*, 23.

4. Genesis 2:4; 5:1; 6:9; 10:1; 11:10, 27; 25:12, 19; 36:1, 9; 37:2.

5. Hamilton, *Book of Genesis*, 29.

6. Melchizedek and Abram both call God "possessor of heaven and earth." The Hebrew term that is often translated "possessor" can also be translated "creator" (see NIV and NRSV, for example) and is cognate to an epithet that appears numerous times in Ugaritic and other Northwest Semitic inscriptions indicating El as creator (see chapter 11).

Chapter 6: What Does It Mean to Whom?

1. See Moran, "Ancient Near Eastern Background of the Love of God in Deuteronomy"; Wright, "Impossible Commandment."

2. Tsumura, *Creation and Destruction*, 34–35.

3. Seely forcefully argues that "*all* peoples in the ancient world thought of the sky as solid" ("The Firmament and the Water Above," 228, emphasis added). In fact, he notes that up to the time of the Renaissance, Jews and Christians discussed the material that made up the sky. As we shall see, the literature of Genesis 1 conforms to the prevailing worldview of Moses' day but not to the theology. Seely's concluding comment is appropriate: "Certainly the historical-grammatical meaning of *raqia'* is 'the ordinary opinion of the writer's day.' Certainly also it is not the purpose of Gen 1:7 to teach us the physical nature of the sky, but to reveal the creator of the sky. Consequently, the reference to the solid firmament 'lies outside the scope of the writer's teachings' and the verse is still infallibly true" (p. 240).

Chapter 7: Genesis 1 Compared with the Egyptian Context

1. Israel struggled with the gods of Egypt from the time of the golden calf incident (shortly after they left Egypt) and throughout their history (Jeroboam made golden calves for Bethel and Dan in the northern kingdom and related them to the golden calf of the Exodus [1 Kings 12:28]). Even in the time of Jeremiah, God was warning the Jews living in Egypt to stop their idolatry (Jer. 44). From the way Exodus 3:14 reveals the name of Yahweh, Stuart supposes that "the generation after Jacob and all subsequent generations up to his own had lost at least a measure—and probably, over time, a greater and greater measure—of the knowledge of the true God and therefore, presumably, of the practice of praying to him and worshiping him regularly and properly, by his name" (Stuart, *Exodus*, 120).

2. For more on this issue, see Morenz, *Egyptian Religion*, 160; Hoffmeier, "Some Thoughts on Genesis 1 and 2 and Egyptian Cosmology," 42; Allen, *Genesis in Egypt*; Wilson, "Egypt," 53–54.

3. Allen, *Genesis in Egypt*, 56.

4. According to other traditions, Ptah (the personification of primal matter and

craftsman god) or Amun (god of wind, representing the essential and hidden) brought Atum into existence. Basically, whichever god is seen as preeminent for the city and time becomes the creator.

5. The connection with the "Spirit" of God in Genesis 1:2 will be clarified below.

6. In fact, creation in Egyptian accounts can be understood as creation of the gods, since every aspect of creation is related to the gods. The biblical text, then, presented a clear and dramatic difference (and polemic).

7. Or, in other traditions, after the first hillock was formed.

8. Re, Amun, or the eye of Atum.

9. Allen, *Genesis in Egypt*, 62.

10. This is in the Memphite Theology, an Egyptian text that describes the creative activity of Ptah and was placed in his temple by Pharaoh Shabaqo. Ptah, the patron god of artisans, was important because he was the god of Memphis. This text is dated to the Nineteenth Dynasty of Egypt, or about 1300 to 1200 B.C. (Allen, "From the 'Memphite Theology,'" 1:21–22).

11. The *ka* is a complex idea in Egyptian thought that does not have a precise equivalent today (Bolshakov, "Ka"). Walton summarizes it as the "vital force" and often it is related to the "spirit" (Walton, *Genesis*, 15). With regard to the gods, however, the ka was usually related to the representation or image of the god (Bolshakov, "Ka," 215).

12. Translated by Allen, "From the 'Memphite Theology,'" 1:23, cols. 58–61.

13. Ibid., 1:23n21.

14. This expression occurs regularly, see Allen, "From the 'Book of Nut,'" 1:6, especially texts J–K and H, "to the winged scarab at Nut's thigh."

15. Allen, "From Coffin Texts Spell 335 = Book of the Dead Spell 17," 1:15–17, especially n18.

16. Allen, *Genesis in Egypt*.

17. Hermopolis was one of the regional administrative centers of ancient Egypt and one of the four main religious centers producing texts dealing with creation. While we do not know of a unified text from Hermopolis on the creation events, there are numerous passages in the Pyramid Texts and Coffin Texts describing aspects of their beliefs. See Sayce, "Egyptian Background,"

241. For a brief description of the Hermopolitan Cosmogony and the Memphite Theology, see Clifford, *Creation Accounts*, 110–14.

18. Gordon Johnston has given a very helpful summary and correlation of this data in "Genesis 1 and Ancient Egyptian Creation Myths."

19. Tsumura argues forcefully that the Hebrew in Genesis 1:2 is better translated "desolate and empty," which fits the Egyptian picture of the precreation chaos very well (*Creation and Destruction*, 9–35).

20. The qualities of the precreation or primordial waters are described in Coffin Text 76, describing Atum's creation of the void as "out of the Flood, out of the Waters, out of the Darkness, out of the Chaos" (Allen, *Genesis in Egypt*, 18; Allen, "From Coffin Texts Spell 76," 1:10, CTII 3d–4d). They are distinguished from the created world by these four terms, defining the primordial waters to be "watery (*nwj*), vs. the 'dryness' (*šw*) of the world; infinite in expanse (*HHw*), vs. the world's 'limits' (*drw*); darkness (*kkw*), vs. light; and *tnmw*, an abstract from the verb *tnm* 'become lost, go astray,' probably referring to the chaotic or unknowable nature of the waters, in contrast to the order and tangibility of creation" (Allen, "From Coffin Texts Spell 76," 1:10n10). Wilson noted the similarities of the initial creative conditions with Genesis 1:2, suggesting that those conditions (represented by four pairs of gods as early as the Middle Kingdom) embodied the four perceived qualities of precreation chaos: "Hūh and Amūn, boundlessness and imperceptibility, are rough parallels to the Hebrew *tohu wavohu*, 'waste and void'; while Kūk, darkness, and Nūn, the abyss, are clearly similar to the Hebrew *hoshek al-penei tehom*, 'darkness upon the face of the deep waters'" (Wilson, "Egypt: The Nature of the Universe," 61). The four pairs of gods, referred to as the Ogdoad, personify the primeval ocean's qualities, boundlessness and darkness (Morenz, *Egyptian Religion*, 175). Hoffmeier also sees the similarity with Genesis 1, but modifies it slightly from Wilson's analysis, suggesting that the term *HHw* relates to both of the two Hebrew terms for "formless and void" and the term *tnmw* (later replaced with the deity Amun) relates to the "Spirit of God" in Genesis 1:2, but should be translated as the "wind of God" (see below and chapter 5; Hoffmeier, "Some Thoughts on Genesis 1 and 2 and Egyptian Cosmology," 43–44).

21. Allen, *Genesis in Egypt*, 7, emphasis added.

22. Ross, *Fingerprint of God*, 165–68.

23. Waltke and Fredricks, *Genesis*, 47. While this particular understanding of the relationship and significance is not crucial to our understanding of Genesis 1, we do believe that it best fits both the biblical text and the cultural background.

24. As we will see in chapter 9, this precreation condition goes beyond merely Egypt's perception and includes Mesopotamia and probably Canaan as well.

25. Sayce, "Egyptian Background," 421.

26. Ibid., 420. Amun is conceived as the creator, for example, in Papyrus Leiden I 350 (Allen, "From Papyrus Leiden I 350," 1:23–26).

27. Hoffmeier, "Some Thoughts on Genesis 1 and 2 and Egyptian Cosmology," 44. Since "Amun originally was the god of wind," it makes a strong parallel and, coupled with the previous four qualities, may even point to a New Kingdom time period (1570–1100 B.C.), which coincides with Israel's sojourn and exodus (ibid.).

28. The basic meaning of the Hebrew term *rûaH* ("blowing" or "wind") comes from the energy and movement of something that cannot be seen. The term, then, referred to the wind, but it then could refer to the breath of a person. It was then extended to the character or nature of the person himself, and finally to the seat of his knowledge and will ("spirit") (Van Pelt, Kaiser, and Block, "רוּחַ," 1073–78).

29. Many commentators deal with this difficult problem. For a brief discussion and suggestion of intentional ambiguity, see Mathews, *Genesis 1–11:26*, 136–37; Wenham, *Genesis 1–15*, 16–17; Walton, *Genesis*, 74–78.

30. See, e.g., Coffin Texts Spell 647 (Allen, "From Coffin Texts Spell 647," 1:18n5) and the Memphite Theology (Allen, "From the 'Memphite Theology,'" 1:22n11).

31. Wilson, "Egypt: The Nature of the Universe," 66–67. According to Allen, creation by spoken word actually predates the Memphite Theology, going back at least to the Coffin Texts (eight hundred years earlier), relating to Atum (alone) as well as Ptah (later): "it describes the means through which Atum effected his own development, by 'surveying in his heart' (Text 9, 18)

and realizing the concept through 'the speech of that august self-developing god' (Text 5, 56)" (*Genesis in Egypt*, 46).

32. However, Morenz suggests that the divine command is later than the other means (*Egyptian Religion*, 163–64), which may make it more prevalent during the time of Israel's Egyptian experience.

33. Allen, *Genesis in Egypt*, 38.

34. Morenz states it this way: "We must realize that in a sacrosanct monarchy people automatically carried into effect the commands given to them," showing the rule of the monarch (*Egyptian Religion*, 165).

35. Hoffmeier, "Some Thoughts on Genesis 1 and 2 and Egyptian Cosmology," 45.

36. Atwell, "An Egyptian Source for Genesis 1," 457. The same tension that the biblical account shows in light appearing before the sun, Atwell finds in the Egyptian tension of identifying Re with Atum as creator and being born daily of Nut.

37. Hoffmeier, "Some Thoughts on Genesis 1 and 2," 44–45. In contrast, however, light is also presented in some texts as being created by the elemental gods of the earthly world after the creation of the land, bringing order to the new world, though still occurring before the sunrise (Morenz, *Egyptian Religion*, 176). Johnston summarizes several of the texts indicating light before the sun in an atmosphere ("Genesis 1 and Ancient Egyptian Creation Myths," 186). The same phenomenon will occur in the Mesopotamian literature in which light seems to be a separate aspect of creation apart from the luminaries (Horowitz, *Mesopotamian Cosmic Geography*, 139).

38. Allen, "From Coffin Texts Spell 76," 1:10; Allen, "From Coffin Texts Spell 80," 1:11–14.

39. Allen, *Genesis in Egypt*, 18–19, 24.

40. Morenz, *Egyptian Religion*, 173–74.

41. See note 3 above in chapter 6 for a discussion of the firmament.

42. Allen, "From a Ramesside Stela," 1:20.

43. Clifford, *Creation Accounts*, 105–6.

44. Allen, *Genesis in Egypt*, 25.

45. Hoffmeier, "Some Thoughts on Genesis 1 and 2 and Egyptian Cosmology," 46–48; Morenz, *Egyptian Religion*, 161, 84–85.

46. Lichtheim, "The Instruction Addressed to King Merikare," *Ancient Egyptian Literature*, 106, lines 131–36. The text presents a "royal instruction" of a king to his son, Merikare, who will reign over Egypt in the Ninth or Tenth Dynasty or about the twenty-first century B.C. The hymn to the creator god forms the climax of the instruction (Lichtheim, "Instruction," 97–98).

47. See Allen, "From Papyrus Bremner-Rhind," 1:15, cols. 27, 2–4; Allen, "From Coffin Texts Spell 80," 1:12, CT II 32b–35h.

48. Lichtheim, "Instruction," 106, lines 136–37.

49. Lichtheim, "Instruction," 106.

50. Atwell, "An Egyptian Source for Genesis 1," 464.

51. Atwell paraphrases the comparison as "harmonious, ordered, complete and satisfying" (ibid., 465).

52. Allen, "From the 'Memphite Theology,'" 1:23, cols. 58–61.

53. Atwell, "An Egyptian Source for Genesis 1," 458.

54. Clifford, *Creation Accounts*, 100.

55. Exodus 6:6–7 emphasizes God's purpose in teaching his people his rule over them and his role in freeing them; Exodus 7:3–5 emphasizes teaching the Egyptians of the sovereign power of Yahweh; and Exodus 9:14–16 emphasizes that the whole world will know Yahweh and his power.

56. For similar lists of the Hermopolitan texts and Memphite Theology that inspired this summary, see Johnston, "Genesis 1 and Ancient Egyptian Creation Myths," 183–84.

57. Currid, *Ancient Egypt and the Old Testament*, 72. See also Atwell's similar conclusion in "An Egyptian Source for Genesis," 466.

Chapter 8: Genesis 1 Distinguished from the Egyptian Context

1. Ryken, Wilhoit, and Longman, *Dictionary of Biblical Imagery*, s.v. "Cosmology."

2. Sayce, "Egyptian Background," 421.

3. Allen, "From the 'Memphite Theology,'" 1:22, lines 55–56: "...but the Ennead is teeth and lips in this mouth that pronounced the identity of everything, and from which Shu and Tefnut emerged and gave birth to the Ennead."

4. Hasel, "Polemic Nature of the Genesis Cosmology," 90.

5. Oswalt argues that the Genesis account is unique because the Egyptian concept still presents creation as an emanation from the god (*The Bible Among the Myths*, 69n8). Clifford agrees that the cause is not significantly different in the Egyptian perception (word or physical emanation; Clifford, *Creation Accounts*, 106). While this may be true, it does not negate the allusion and in fact makes the point: Genesis takes a common perception of creation and invests it with a new understanding of the Creator.

6. Johnston, "Genesis 1 and Ancient Egyptian Creation Myths," 187.

7. Clifford, *Creation Accounts*, 106.

8. Allen, "From the 'Memphite Theology,'" 1:23, lines 59–62.

9. Waltke and Fredricks, *Genesis*, 71–72.

10. John Oswalt argues forcefully for the dramatic difference in the presentation of God through Genesis and the biblical accounts in comparison to the mythical thinking of the rest of the ancient Near East (*The Bible Among the Myths*).

11. Futato, "Because It Had Rained," 14, 20.

12. Morenz, *Egyptian Religion*, 167.

13. Ibid., 168.

14. For a helpful summary of the Egyptian understanding of the daily cycle, see ibid., 166–71.

15. Ibid., 168.

16. Plumley, "Cosmology of Ancient Egypt," 39.

17. Allen, *Genesis in Egypt*, 7.

18. Morenz, *Egyptian Religion*, 166.

19. See chapter 5, under "Israel's Historical Circumstances."

20. Tsumura, *Creation and Destruction*, 140.

Chapter 9: Genesis 1 Compared with the Mesopotamian Context

1. These come from both Sumerian and Akkadian texts (Clifford, *Creation Accounts*, 13–98).

2. Enuma Elish is generally dated to the latter part of the second millennium B.C. (Foster, *Before the Muses*, 1:350).

3. Creation of the cosmos is also attributed to Anu, Enlil, and Ea; Ea, Tiamat,

and Apsu all create gods; the creation of people is also attributed to Anu, Enlil, Ninhursag, and Ea; etc.

4. Clifford, *Creation Accounts*, 71–73.

5. Apsu and Tiamat represent the initial freshwater and saltwater bodies and exist at the beginning of Enuma Elish (Horowitz, *Mesopotamian Cosmic Geography*, 109). Another account of creation to justify Marduk's position as king, "The Chaldean Cosmogony" (or the Eridu Story of Creation or Eridu Genesis, dating to about 600 B.C.) begins the creation with "all the lands were sea" (Clifford, *Creation Accounts*, 63, line 10). On this sea, Marduk built land as a floating island and populated it with man, animals, and everything they needed. The initial condition of watery mass seems to be assumed consistently.

6. The lack of combat or struggle in creation is illustrated by "The Chaldean Cosmogony" (Clifford, *Creation Accounts*, 62–64).

7. Heidel, *Babylonian Genesis*, 101.

8. Foster, "Epic of Creation," 1:397, tablet 4, lines 22–26, see n6.

9. Ibid., 1:397–99.

10. Clifford, *Creation Accounts*, 63. Another account simply states that "the earth had been fashioned" ("Another Account of the Creation of Man," in Heidel, *Babylonian Genesis*, 68, line 3).

11. Foster, "Epic of Creation," 1:391, tablet 1, line 50.

12. Ibid., line 2.

13. Horowitz cites a Sumerian fragmentary text from Nippur, NBC 11108, which seems to be addressing the period of time just before and after the first acts of creation (*Mesopotamian Cosmic Geography*, 139).

14. Tsumura argues effectively that the idea of separating the waters is similar, but that the biblical account is neither necessarily indebted to Enuma Elish, nor assumes a cosmic conflict as the background for this separation (like the battle between Marduk and Tiamat) (*Creation and Destruction*, 36–53).

15. Clifford, *Creation Accounts*, 31; Farber, "The Song of the Hoe," 1:511, lines 4–5.

16. Heidel, *Babylonian Genesis*, 115.

17. Foster, "Epic of Creation," 1:399, lines 1–24.

18. Clifford, *Creation Accounts*, 68.

19. Foster, "Atra-Hasis," 1:451, lines 224–29. In *Enuma Elish*, Marduk proposes making man from the blood of Qingu, but clay is not specifically mentioned (Foster, "Epic of Creation," 1:400, tablet 6, lines 5–8).

20. Clifford, *Creation Accounts*, 30–31.

21. Foster, "Epic of Creation," 1:397, tablet 4, lines 43–46; 1:399, tablet 5, lines 3–4, 20–24; 1:401, tablet 6, lines 51–54.

22. Walton, *Lost World of Genesis One*, presents this thesis as the main argument of his book in the first nine chapters.

23. Walton, *Lost World*, "Proposition 9," 87–92.

24. For comparison, see Heidel, *Babylonian Genesis*, 129.

25. Clifford, *Creation Accounts*, 62–63; Heidel, *Babylonian Genesis*, 64, 117.

26. Clifford, *Creation Accounts*, 55–58.

27. Heidel, *Babylonian Genesis*, 132–39. Tsumura summarizes the view that "it is not correct to say that 'Enuma Elish' was adopted and adapted by the Israelites to produce the Genesis stories" ("Genesis and Ancient Near Eastern Stories," 32). While Lambert generally agrees with this, he does see a precedent for the Sabbath in Atrahasis ("A New Look," 106–7). Heidel identifies and examines three options with respect to dependence: that Mesopotamia borrowed from Moses, Moses borrowed from Mesopotamia, or they both had an earlier source from which they took basic ideas. He asserts that only the third can hold up under scrutiny (*Babylonian Genesis*, 130–39). We are supposing a modification of the third view—that Moses may be using general ideas common to Israel's neighbors, ancient Near Eastern ways of describing creation, and cultural milieu without challenge, while challenging the nature and activity of God.

Chapter 10: Genesis 1 Distinguished from the Mesopotamian Context

1. For a good discussion of the issue, see chapter 2, "The Waters in Genesis 1," in Tsumura, *Creation and Destruction*, 36–57.

2. Heidel, *Babylonian Genesis*, 126–27.

3. Foster, "Epic of Creation," 1:396–97, lines 1–30, see n6.

4. Heidel, *Babylonian Genesis*, 126.

5. See chapter 7, "Means of Creation."

6. Light was not tied to the luminaries in Mesopotamian perception (Horowitz, *Mesopotamian Cosmic Geography*, 139). See also chapter 9.

7. It is true that God is often metaphorically described in terms of light ("God is light, and in him is no darkness at all," 1 John 1:5). This metaphor, however, does not describe light as an attribute of God but compares God to light in significant ways for the particular context in which the metaphor is used.

8. The first four tablets (out of seven) in Enuma Elish are devoted to this battle and the preparations for it. See Foster, "Epic of Creation," 1:390–402.

9. Tsumura's *Creation and Destruction* demonstrates the lack of this theme.

10. Clifford, *Creation Accounts*, 71.

11. In "The Chaldean Cosmogony" (Clifford, *Creation Accounts*, 62, line 18).

12. In "The Worm and the Toothache" (ibid., 55, line 2).

13. Psalm 95 presents the Creator God who is worthy of worship, which is equated with rest. Those who do not serve God cannot enter his rest, but by implication, those who worship and so serve him in loyalty do enter his rest. Hebrews 4 picks up the same theme and encourages all believers to enter into God's rest through obedience (4:1–13). Obedient service to God in worship is the gateway to enjoying the rest of God. This helps us to understand the injunction to the Israelites to observe a tangible day of rest. In imitating God, they are paying obedient homage to him as creator and sharing his rest.

14. Foster, "Epic of Creation," 1:300, line 8.

15. See "Proposition 7: Divine Rest Is in a Temple," in Walton, *Lost World of Genesis One*, 72–77.

16. See the discussion, especially, on Exodus 31:17 in chapter 4.

17. The garden in Eden is probably meant to be understood as a temple, comparable to the ultimate temple in the end of Revelation, a temple in which mankind will worship and serve. Such a picture of the garden does not diminish the purpose of God in providing for the well-being of his image bearer. In fact, the focus of the garden is for man's benefit, not God's.

18. Clifford, *Creation Accounts*, 71.

19. See chapter 12, "But Wouldn't It Be Misleading for God to Say Creation Occurred in Seven Days If It Really Didn't?"

20. Ibid., 71.

21. The Egyptians gods are presented as having a sort of transcendence (in some sense independent of creation and preexisting in the sense of creating themselves; e.g., Ptah or Atum), yet also very much a part of creation itself (Allen, *Genesis in Egypt*, 48–50). This is still very different from the biblical conception of God's transcendence. The Mesopotamian accounts present no sense of transcendence among their gods. Oswalt (*The Bible Among the Myths*) argues forcefully for the uniqueness of God in the Bible compared to the ancient Near Eastern accounts of their gods.

Chapter 11: Genesis 1 and the Canaanite Context

1. See Clifford, *Creation Accounts*, 118–19.

2. For example, the inscriptions at Kuntillet ʿAjrud and Khirbet el-Qom mention both Yahweh and Asherah together, possibly as consorts (Hess, *Israelite Religions*, 283–90). This really comes as no surprise when reading the book of Judges, the historical books, or the Prophets, and hearing their constant denouncing of Israel's idolatry.

3. Clifford, *Creation Accounts*, 132.

4. Tsumura (*Creation and Destruction*) argues effectively that the relevant passages in the Hebrew Bible do not include the element of cosmic conflict.

5. Futato, "Because It Had Rained," 1–21.

6. For example, Anat, Astarte, Baal, and Qedeshet are known in Egyptian iconography and accompanying texts from the time of the exodus (Cornelius, *Many Faces of the Goddess*, 69–70). In fact, Anat had been "received into the family of Egyptian deities at the beginning of the Nineteenth Dynasty" or about the beginning of the thirteenth century B.C. She was even claimed by the pharaoh for protection (Shupak, "New Light on Shamgar Ben ʿAnath," 519).

7. Averbeck, "Three 'Daughters' of Baal."

8. Ibid., 9.

9. Futato, "Because It Had Rained," 18–21.

Chapter 12: Objections (Part 1)

1. You may argue that God finally did correct their wrong view of marriage, which is true. At least correction is clearly implied in Jesus' words of Matthew 19:5, "hold fast to his [one] wife." And it is implied in the qualifications for an elder or deacon (1 Tim. 3:2, 12; "husband of one wife"). But these corrections do not come until thousands of years after Israel's beginning of polygamy! God does not clearly correct the social disorder of slavery. The New Testament Scriptures show that slaves and free are equal in the kingdom of God (Gal. 3:28; 1 Cor. 12:13), but do not say to free slaves or that it is wrong to hold them. We recognize the disorder now as we have processed the theology of man's image and value before God.

2. This is the main point for Futato, "Because It Had Rained."

3. Hasel, "Polemic Nature," 91.

4. Averbeck, "Three 'Daughters' of Baal."

5. This problem is well described and addressed by Walton (*Ancient Near Eastern Thought*, 36).

6. Younger, "The Old Testament in Its Cultural Context," 80–84.

7. Erickson and Hustad, *Introducing Christian Doctrine*, 72.

8. Ibid., with illustrations on 72–74.

9. This would be very similar to the use of "phenomenal" language rather than technical language. In other words, it is communicating according to what the speaker and/or reader assumes to be true (or speaks as if it is true) because of their observations. See number 4 in Erickson's list of principles (ibid., 73).

10. Atwell, "An Egyptian Source for Genesis 1," 472–73. On the other hand, Gordon Johnston ("Genesis 1 and Ancient Egyptian Creation Myths") has drawn attention to two texts that include a "seven days" motif in the creation of man ("Creation of Man by Mother Goddess") and the world ("Adapa"), but neither of these presents creation as occurring in seven days. At the 2006 Evangelical Theological Society meeting in Washington, DC, where Johnston first presented this paper, he included a helpful appendix entitled "Six//Seven Day Structure of Genesis 1:1–2:3 as Polemic Against One-Day Structure of Egyptian Creation Mythology," where he collected a number of

usages of seven days in ancient writings. When his paper was published, the appendix was not included.

11. See above note regarding Johnston's appendix A.

12. It actually occurs several times as a pattern of three sets of two days with a climactic seventh. So, for example, in the ʾAqhatu Legend, Dani'ilu gives food and drink to the gods for three sets of two days until Baal appears on the seventh day and intercedes (Pardee, "The ʾAqhatu Legend," 1:343–44, lines 5–18).

13. The pattern occurs repeatedly in "The Kirta Epic" (Pardee, 1:333–43).

14. See, e.g., the Babylonian equivalent to the Noah story when the ship stops on the mountain before sending out a dove (Foster, "Gilgamesh," 1:458–60). Seven days is also the length of the flood in Atrahasis (Foster, "Atra-Hasis," 1:450–53) and the building of Baal's palace in the Baʿlu myth (Pardee, "The Baʿlu Myth," 1:241–74). The use of seven days occurs frequently with many more examples.

15. The number seven can be used to indicate a large or indefinite number. Kapelrud argues from the Ugaritic material that it is commonly symbolic and intended to be understood not literally but rather as *complete* or *full* or *maximum*. With regard to time, it can indicate "intensity, more than duration. That can be seen again and again in the texts" (Kapelrud, "The Number Seven in Ugaritic Texts," 498).

16. Tobin, "Mythological Texts," 459.

17. The term *sabbath* itself may be related to "the Babylonian term *šapattu*, meaning the completion of the moon's waxing, i.e., the fifteenth day of a lunar month" (Lambert, "New Look," 106). The concept of a seventh day of rest, unrelated to the lunar calendar, however, is unique to Israel. In fact, Israel's use of the seven-day week seems to be unique in the ancient world (Wells, "Exodus," 232–33).

18. As mentioned previously, John Walton has suggested that the seven days refer to the dedication of God's cosmic temple; his proposal recognizes the ancient Near Eastern background in which the gods typically rest in their temples (*Lost World of Genesis One*, 72–77). With a similar argument, Kline suggests that the Sabbath rest indicates the completion of the temple

and Yahweh's enthronement and rule (*Kingdom Prologue*, 19, 33–41). The Scriptures clearly refer to all of creation as the temple of God (Isa. 66:1; Ps. 11:4) and the temple of God as his resting place (2 Chron. 6:41–42; Ps. 132:7–8). The framing of the narrative in seven days would not be intended to reflect a time frame for creation, but rather, as with the ancient Near Eastern parallels, a theological statement of God's rule from his dedicated temple, and in Walton's case in *Lost World*, a literal seven days of dedication of the temple. In the case of Kline, the seven days describe the construction of the temple with Yahweh's subsequent enthronement and rule over his creation. In this case, Kline would see the seven days as figurative and nonchronological (*Kingdom Prologue*, 29–35).

19. For further reading on the issues of chronology in Judges, see Block, *Judges, Ruth*, 59–63; Younger, *Judges and Ruth*, 24–25.

20. An additional example would include 2 Kings 18–20. Further, while they are not all narrative, none of the Major Prophets are chronological.

21. Heidel (*Babylonian Genesis*, 139) cites this suggestion from Price, *The Monuments and the Old Testament*, 129–30.

Chapter 13: Objections (Part 2)

1. The Hebrew text reads *beyom*, literally, "in the day," as the NASB translates it. It has the sense of "when," and is translated thus in many translations (e.g., NIV, NLT). Because of this, Jonathan Sarfati argues that this text does not reflect a nonliteral use of the word *yom*, because it means something other than a day (*Refuting Compromise*, 70–71). He correctly calls it idiomatic, but he recognizes that his understanding must be supported y context. Rather, we would say that it shows that *yom* has other meanings than a twenty-four-hour day, even within the very context of the creation week. In fact, if the week of creation had been a literal week, the text could easily have said, "in the *week* that the Lord God made heaven and earth." However, some scholars argue that this is indeed speaking of a single day and refers to the following creation account in Genesis 2 as occurring in just one day (Carlson and Longman, *Science, Creation, and the Bible*, 118–19).

2. Our concern is not to argue for "day" as a figurative day or long period of

time. Rather, it is to show that the argument for a necessary literalism is misplaced. We have already argued that Genesis is presenting a week that is symbolic as a whole, not a literal week.

3. Neither of the standard Hebrew lexicons (*The Brown-Driver-Briggs Hebrew and English Lexicon* [commonly abbreviated BDB] or *The Hebrew and Aramaic Lexicon of the Old Testament* [commonly abbreviated HALOT]) analyzes this form as a homonym, though that might be the natural expectation. They suggest it is a distinct meaning of the same word in Hebrew.

4. The same terminology is used in Daniel 8:14: "For 2,300 evenings and mornings . . . ," does not seem to refer to literal days. Instead, it seems to refer historically to half the number of days—3 years and 55 days (1,150 days), not 6 years and 110 days (2,300 days). Cf. Archer, "Daniel," 102–3. Ironically, in both Daniel 8:14 and 8:26, "evenings and mornings" is actually singular in the Hebrew ("evening and morning"). Probably this use of the singular should be understood as a collective, but it may also urge caution on our understanding of the use of the phrase.

5. At least some Young Earth Creationists, such as Jonathan Sarfati, allow death before the fall for plants and invertebrates, arguing that the curse only affected the *"nephesh chayyah"* ("breath of life"), which Sarfati assumes refers to only vertebrates (*Refuting Compromise*, 205).

6. Mathews, *Genesis 1–11:26*, 211.

7. Even if we take the passage literally, yet argue that the death is primarily spiritual death (since they did not die immediately), it would be difficult to argue for a spiritual life (eternal life?) since God denies them access to the tree after the fall. He does not deny access to spiritual life, only to perpetual physical existence.

8. Murray, *The Epistle to the Romans in Two Volumes*, 181.

9. After stating that disease, death, viruses, and bacteria "were modifications to [God's] perfect creation brought about because of sin," Dennis Lindsay states, "Romans 8:22 declares that the whole creation groans under the load of sin. In other words, disease, death and decay are not only a burden, but also a way of life for the entire creation on account of man's sin" (*Harmony of Science and Scripture*, 155–56). He goes on to state that "the law of decay now

in operation [is] due to the fall of man" (159). To their credit, not all Young Earth Creationists hold to a change in the physical laws. Sarfati, for instance, argues for a special sustaining power of God before the fall, though he still argues for the absence of death before the fall from this passage (*Refuting Compromise*, 213–14).

10. Murray, *Epistle to the Romans*, 301–2. See also Cranfield, *Critical and Exegetical Commentary*, 413–14.

11. Cranfield, *A Critical and Exegetical Commentary on the Epistle to the Romans*, 414.

Chapter 14: Toward a Creation Theology

1. Tsumura, *Creation and Destruction*, 9–35.

2. For further reading on this difficult but very important concept, consult Blocher, *In the Beginning*, chapter 4; Waltke and Fredricks, *Genesis*, 65–66.

3. Cf. Genesis 2:15. The Hebrew text of this verse could be translated "for keeping and serving." Both of these terms are used extensively in the Pentateuch for worship and service to Yahweh. In this context, however, the keeping seems to have a protective element (see the immediate context of the threat in Gen. 3 and the similar use of the term in 3:24 where the cherubim "kept" or guarded the way back to the Tree of Life), and the serving focuses on service to the king through the maintenance of the garden (see Gen. 2:5 and the problem of no man to "work" or "cultivate" the ground, in which the same term relates to the means of providing for the Great King's land). If we see the garden as an earthly temple for Yahweh, serving in it becomes a tangible expression of worship!

4. Walton, *Lost World of Genesis One*. Whether he is correct or not, God's rest would be perceived in the ancient world in the context of his temple.

Chapter 15: The End of Debate?

1. Personal email from a friend, September 14, 2007.

BIBLIOGRAPHY

Allen, James P. "From a Ramesside Stela." In Hallo and Younger, *Context*, § 1.13, p. 20.

―――. "From Coffin Texts Spell 76." In Hallo and Younger, *Context*, § 1.6, pp. 10–11.

―――. "From Coffin Texts Spell 80." In Hallo and Younger, *Context*, § 1.8, pp. 11–14.

―――. "From Coffin Texts Spell 335 = Book of the Dead Spell 17." In Hallo and Younger, *Context*, § 1.10, pp. 15–17.

―――. "From Coffin Texts Spell 647." In Hallo and Younger, *Context*, § 1.12, pp. 18–19.

―――. "From Papyrus Bremner-Rhind." In Hallo and Younger, *Context*, § 1.9, pp. 14–15.

―――. "From Papyrus Leiden I 350." In Hallo and Younger, *Context*, § 1.16, pp. 23–26.

―――. "From the 'Book of Nut.'" In Hallo and Younger, *Context*, § 1.1, pp. 5–6.

―――. "From the 'Memphite Theology.'" In Hallo and Younger, *Context*, § 1.15, pp. 21–23.

―――. *Genesis in Egypt: The Philosophy of Ancient Egyptian Creation Accounts*, Yale Egyptological Studies 2. New Haven, CT: Yale Egyptological Seminar, Dept. of Near Eastern Languages and Civilizations, Graduate School, Yale University, 1988.

Archer, Gleason L. "Daniel." In *The Expositor's Bible Commentary*, edited by Frank E. Gaebelein. Grand Rapids: Zondervan, 1985.

Atwell, James E. "An Egyptian Source for Genesis 1." *Journal of Theological Studies* 51, no. 2 (2000): 441–77.

Averbeck, Richard E. "The Three 'Daughters' of Baal and Transformations of Chaoskampf in the Early Chapters of Genesis." Midwest American Oriental Society Annual Meeting Plenary Address, February 11, 2011.

Bailey, Kenneth Ewing. *Poet and Peasant: A Literary Cultural Approach to the Parables in Luke*. Grand Rapids: Eerdmans, 1976.

Blocher, Henri. *In the Beginning: The Opening Chapters of Genesis*. Leicester, England; Downers Grove, IL: InterVarsity Press, 1984.

Block, Daniel Isaac. *Judges, Ruth*, The New American Commentary. Nashville: Broadman & Holman, 1999.

Bolshakov, Andrey O. "Ka." In *The Oxford Encyclopedia of Ancient Egypt*. Edited by Donald B. Redford, 215–17. New York: Oxford University Press, 2001.

Boyd, Gregory A., and Paul R. Eddy. *Across the Spectrum: Understanding Issues in Evangelical Theology*. 2nd ed. Grand Rapids: Baker Academic, 2009.

Carlson, Richard F., and Tremper Longman. *Science, Creation, and the Bible: Reconciling Rival Theories of Origins*. Downers Grove, IL: InterVarsity Press, 2010.

Cassuto, Umberto. *A Commentary on the Book of Genesis, Part 1*. Publications of the Perry Foundation for Biblical Research in the Hebrew University of Jerusalem. Jerusalem: Magnes Press Hebrew University, 1998.

Clifford, Richard J. *Creation Accounts in the Ancient Near East and the Bible*. The Catholic Biblical Quarterly. Monograph Series 26. Washington, DC: Catholic Biblical Association, 1994.

Collins, Francis S. *The Language of God: A Scientist Presents Evidence for Belief*. New York: Free Press, 2006.

Cornelius, Izak. *The Many Faces of the Goddess: The Iconography of the*

Syro-Palestinian Goddesses Anat, Astarte, Qedeshet, and Asherah C. 1500–1000 BCE. Orbis Biblicus Et Orientalis. Fribourg: Academic Press: Vandenhoeck & Ruprecht, 2004.

Cranfield, C. E. B. *A Critical and Exegetical Commentary on the Epistle to the Romans.* 6th ed. Vol. 1. The International Critical Commentary. Edinburgh: Clark, 1975.

Currid, John D. *Ancient Egypt and the Old Testament.* Grand Rapids: Baker, 1997.

Erickson, Millard J. *Introducing Christian Doctrine.* Edited by L. Arnold Hustad. 2nd ed. Grand Rapids: Baker, 2001.

Farber, Gertrud, trans. "The Song of the Hoe." In Hallo and Younger, *Context,* § 1.157, pp. 511–13.

Foster, Benjamin R. *Before the Muses: An Anthology of Akkadian Literature.* 2nd ed. Potomac, MD: CDL Press, 1996.

————, trans. "Atra-Hasis." In Hallo and Younger, *Context,* § 1.130, pp. 450–53.

————, trans. "Epic of Creation." In Hallo and Younger, *Context,* § 1.111, pp. 390–402.

————, trans. "Gilgamesh." In Hallo and Younger, *Context,* § 1.132, pp. 458–60.

Futato, Mark D. "Because It Had Rained: A Study of Gen 2:5–7 with Implications for Gen 2:4–25 and Gen 1:1–2:3." *Westminster Theological Journal* 60, no. 1 (1998): 1–21.

Galilei, Galileo. "Letter to the Grand Duchess Christina of Tuscany, 1615." Modern History Sourcebook. Fordham University. http://www.fordham.edu/halsall/mod/galileo-tuscany.html.

Garrett, Duane A. *Rethinking Genesis: The Sources and Authorship of the First Book of the Pentateuch.* Grand Rapids: Baker, 1991.

Hallo, William W., and K. Lawson Younger Jr., eds. *Context of Scripture.* 3 vols. Leiden; Boston: Brill, 2003.

Hamilton, Victor P. *The Book of Genesis: Chapters 1–17.* The New International Commentary on the Old Testament. Grand Rapids: Eerdmans, 1990.

Hartnett, John W. *Starlight, Time and the New Physics: How We Can See Starlight in Our Young Universe*. Creation Ministries International. Eight Mile Plains, Queensland, Australia: Creation Book Publishers, 2007.

Hasel, Gerhard F. "Polemic Nature of the Genesis Cosmology." *Evangelical Quarterly* 46 (1974): 81–102.

Heidel, Alexander. *The Babylonian Genesis: The Story of Creation*. 2d ed. Chicago: University of Chicago Press, 1963.

Hess, Richard S. *Israelite Religions: An Archaeological and Biblical Survey*. Grand Rapids: Baker, 2007.

Hoffmeier, James K. "Some Thoughts on Genesis 1 and 2 and Egyptian Cosmology." *Journal of the Ancient Near Eastern Society* 15 (1983): 39–49.

Horowitz, Wayne. *Mesopotamian Cosmic Geography*, Mesopotamian Civilizations [8]. Winona Lake, IN: Eisenbrauns, 1998.

Howard, David M. *Joshua*. The New American Commentary. Nashville: Broadman & Holman, 1998.

Hummel, Charles E. *The Galileo Connection: Resolving Conflicts Between Science and the Bible*. Downers Grove, IL: InterVarsity Press, 1986.

Humphreys, D. Russell. *Starlight and Time: Solving the Puzzle of Distant Starlight in a Young Universe*. Green Forest, AR: Master Books, 1994.

Johnston, Gordon H. "Genesis 1 and Ancient Egyptian Creation Myths." *Bibliotheca Sacra* 165, no. 658 (2008): 178–94.

Kapelrud, Arvid S. "The Number Seven in Ugaritic Texts." *Vetus Testamentum* 18, no. 4 (1968): 494–99.

Kline, Meredith G. *Kingdom Prologue: Genesis Foundations for a Covenantal Worldview*. Eugene, OR: Wipf and Stock, 2006.

Koehler, Ludwig, Walter Baumgartner, and Johann Jakob Stamm. *Hebrew and Aramaic Lexicon of the Old Testament*. Translated and edited under the supervision of M. E. J. Richardson. New York: Brill, 1999.

Lambert, W. G. "A New Look at the Babylonian Background of Genesis." In *I Studied Inscriptions from Before the Flood: Ancient Near Eastern, Literary, and Linguistic Approaches to Genesis 1–11*. Edited by Richard S. Hess and David Toshio Tsumura, 96–113. Winona Lake, IN: Eisenbrauns, 1994.

Lichtheim, Miriam. *Ancient Egyptian Literature; a Book of Readings*. Berkeley: University of California Press, 1973.

Lindsay, Dennis Gordon. *Harmony of Science and Scripture*. Creation Science Series 2. Dallas: Christ for the Nations, 1997.

Longman, Tremper. *How to Read Genesis*. Downers Grove, IL: InterVarsity Press, 2005.

Mathews, Kenneth A. *Genesis 1–11:26*. Vol. 1A. New American Commentary. Nashville: Broadman & Holman, 1995.

Moran, William L. "Ancient Near Eastern Background of the Love of God in Deuteronomy." *Catholic Biblical Quarterly* 25, no. 1 (1963): 77–87.

Morenz, Siegfried. *Egyptian Religion*. Ithaca, NY: Cornell University Press, 1973.

Morris, Henry M., ed. *Scientific Creationism* by Institute for Creation Research. Public school ed. San Diego: Creation-Life Publishers, 1974.

Murray, John. *The Epistle to the Romans in Two Volumes*. The New International Commentary on the New Testament. Grand Rapids: Eerdmans, 1959.

Numbers, Ronald L. *The Creationists*. New York: A. A. Knopf, 1992.

Oswalt, John. *The Bible Among the Myths: Unique Revelation or Just Ancient Literature?* Grand Rapids: Zondervan, 2009.

Pardee, Dennis. "The ʾAqhatu Legend." In Hallo and Younger, *Context*, § 1.103, pp. 343–56.

———. "The Baʿlu Myth." In Hallo and Younger, *Context*, § 1.86, pp. 241–74.

———. "The Kirta Epic." In Hallo and Younger, *Context*, § 1.102, pp. 333–43.

Plumley, J. Martin. "The Cosmology of Ancient Egypt." In *Ancient Cosmologies*. Edited by Carmen Blacker and Michael Loewe, 17–41. London: Allen and Unwin, 1975.

Price, Ira Maurice. *The Monuments and the Old Testament: Light from the Near East on the Scriptures*. New rewritten ed. Philadelphia, Boston, etc.: Judson Press, 1925.

Ross, Hugh. *The Fingerprint of God*. 2nd ed. Orange, CA: Promise Publishing Co., 1991.

———. *A Matter of Days: Resolving a Creation Controversy*. Colorado Springs: NavPress, 2004.

Rowland, Wade. *Galileo's Mistake: A New Look at the Epic Confrontation Between Galileo and the Church*. 1st US ed. New York: Arcade, 2003.

Ryken, Leland, James C. Wilhoit, and Tremper Longman, eds. *Dictionary of Biblical Imagery*. Downers Grove, IL: InterVarsity Press., 1998.

Sailhamer, John H. *Genesis*. In *The Expositor's Bible Commentary: Genesis, Exodus, Leviticus, Numbers*. Edited by Frank E. Gaebelein. Grand Rapids: Zondervan, 1990.

Sarfati, Jonathan D. *Refuting Compromise: A Biblical and Scientific Refutation of "Progressive Creationism" (Billions of Years) as Popularized by Astronomer Hugh Ross*. 1st ed. Green Forest, AR: Master Books, 2004.

Sarna, Nahum M. *Genesis: The Traditional Hebrew Text with the New JPS Translation*. The JPS Torah Commentary. Philadelphia: Jewish Publication Society, 1989.

Sayce, A. H. "The Egyptian Background of Genesis I." In *Studies Presented to F. Ll. Griffith*. Edited by S. R. K. Glanville and Nora Macdonald Griffith, 419. London: Egypt Exploration Society H. Milford, Oxford University Press, 1932.

Seely, Paul H. "The Firmament and the Water Above, Part 1: The Meaning of *raqia'* in Gen 1:6–8." *Westminster Theological Journal* 53, no. 2 (1991): 227–40.

Shupak, Nili. "New Light on Shamgar Ben 'Anath." *Biblica* 70, no. 4 (1989): 517–25.

Snoke, David. *A Biblical Case for an Old Earth.* Grand Rapids: Baker, 2006.

Sterchi, David A. "Does Genesis 1 Provide a Chronological Sequence?" *Journal of the Evangelical Theological Society* 39, no. 4 (1996): 529–36.

Stuart, Douglas K. *Exodus.* Edited by Ray Clendenen. Vol. 2. The New American Commentary. Nashville: Broadman & Holman, 2006.

Tobin, Vincent Arieh. "Mythological Texts." In *The Oxford Encyclopedia of Ancient Egypt.* Edited by Donald B. Redford, 459–64. New York: Oxford University Press, 2001.

Tsumura, David Toshio. *Creation and Destruction: A Reappraisal of the Chaoskampf Theory in the Old Testament.* Winona Lake, IN: Eisenbrauns, 2005.

————. "Genesis and Ancient Near Eastern Stories of Creation and Flood: An Introduction." In *I Studied Inscriptions from Before the Flood: Ancient Near Eastern, Literary, and Linguistic Approaches to Genesis 1–11.* Edited by Richard S. Hess and David Toshio Tsumura, 27–57. Winona Lake, IN: Eisenbrauns, 1994.

Van Pelt, M. V., W. C. Kaiser Jr., and D. I. Block. "רוּחַ." In *New International Dictionary of Old Testament Theology and Exegesis.* Edited by Willem VanGemeren, 1073–78. Grand Rapids: Zondervan, 1997.

Waltke, Bruce K., and Cathi J. Fredricks. *Genesis: A Commentary.* Grand Rapids: Zondervan, 2001.

Waltke, Bruce K., and Michael Patrick O'Connor. *An Introduction to Biblical Hebrew Syntax.* Winona Lake, IN: Eisenbrauns, 1990.

Walton, John H. *Ancient Near Eastern Thought and the Old Testament: Introducing the Conceptual World of the Hebrew Bible.* Grand Rapids: Baker, 2006.

————. *Genesis: From Biblical Text . . . To Contemporary Life.* The NIV Application Commentary. Grand Rapids: Zondervan, 2001.

————. *The Lost World of Genesis One: Ancient Cosmology and the Origins Debate.* Downers Grove, IL: InterVarsity Press, 2009.

Wells, Bruce. "Exodus." In *Zondervan Illustrated Bible Backgrounds Commentary.* Edited by John H. Walton. Grand Rapids: Zondervan, 2009.

Wenham, Gordon J. *Genesis 1–15.* Word Biblical Commentary. Dallas: Word Books, 1987.

Whitcomb, John Clement, and Henry M. Morris. *The Genesis Flood: The Biblical Record and Its Scientific Implications.* Philadelphia: Presbyterian and Reformed, 1961.

Wilson, John A. "Egypt: The Nature of the Universe." In *Before Philosophy, the Intellectual Adventure of Ancient Man; an Essay on Speculative Thought in the Ancient Near East.* Edited by Henri Frankfort, H. A. Frankfort, John A. Wilson, and Thorkild Jacobsen, 39–70. Harmondsworth, Middlesex: Penguin Books, 1946. Reprint, 1973.

Wright, J. Edward. "Biblical Versus Israelite Images of the Heavenly Realm." *Journal for the Study of the Old Testament* 93 (2001): 59–75.

Wright, Rebecca Abts. "The Impossible Commandment." *Anglican Theological Review* 83, no. 3 (2001): 579–84.

Younger, K. Lawson. *Judges and Ruth: From Biblical Text . . . To Contemporary Life.* The NIV Application Commentary. Grand Rapids: Zondervan, 2002.

————. "The Old Testament in Its Cultural Context: Implications of 'Contextual Criticism' for Chinese and North American Christian Identity." In *After Imperialism.* Edited by R. R. Cook and D. W. Pao. Eugene, OR: Pickwick/Wipf and Stock, 2011. Pp. 73–95.